The Children You Want
You Want
with the
Kids You Have

Other Books by Marie Calder Ricks

Be Successful in School: A Student's Guide
for Junior High and High School

House of Order Handbook:
The Best Way to an Organized Life

Organize as You Go:
Successful Skills for Busy Lifestyles

Organized for a Mission:
A Guide for Parents and Missionaries

Project Organization:
Quick and Easy Ways to Organize Your Life

The Children You Want

with the

Kids You Have

Training Children to Work and Gain Other Essential Skills

Marie Calder Ricks

DESERET
BOOK

SALT LAKE CITY, UTAH

Visit www.houseoforder.com for information regarding your organizational needs, to purchase organizational products, or to schedule a personal consultation, speaking engagement, or educational seminar.

Quote on page ix from H. David Burton, "More Holiness Give Me," *Ensign,* November 2004, 100.

Text © 2010 Marie Calder Ricks
Illustration on this page © 2010 Thomas E. Ricks

Library of Congress Cataloging-in-Publication Data
Ricks, Marie Calder.
    The children you want with the kids you have / Marie Calder Ricks.
        p. cm.
    Includes index.
    ISBN 978-1-60641-665-5 (pbk.)
    1. Child rearing. I. Title.
    HQ769.R54 2010
    649'.64—dc22   2010011521

Printed in the United States of America
Malloy Lithographing Incorporated, Ann Arbor, MI

10   9   8   7   6   5   4   3   2   1

To Timothy Alan Ricks, our first grandson,
and to all parents, mentors, and teachers who strive for
a better way to influence, guide, and instruct
the children in their care

Contents

Contents

*It is important for families and individuals
to aggressively seek more of the virtues
which go beyond this mortal life.*

*A prayerful, conservative approach is the key
to successfully living in an affluent society and
building the qualities that come from waiting, sharing,
saving, working hard, and making do with what we have.*

*May we be blessed with the desire and the ability
to understand when more is really less
and when more is better.*

—H. David Burton

Introduction

Several years ago I realized that children today are struggling. Most don't seem to know much about waiting, sharing, saving, working hard, or making do. This motivated me to begin studying and writing about raising happier, healthier, hardworking children. Because I do personal coaching and home organization, I am in a lot of homes. I see interactions between parents and children, on both their good days and bad days. I have also visited with clients about their childhood experiences, and I have discovered that much of what they are struggling with now organizationally is due to past (usually negative) experiences when they were children and teenagers.

Often parents themselves didn't feel secure, weren't taught how to work, or didn't have consistent chores. There were not enough firm, understanding adult figures in their lives to make them stick to a job until its completion and then give them validation for the work that was done. Positive experiences didn't happen frequently enough to form pleasant "chore memories" and consistent work habits, even in otherwise model families. As children, they were not given sufficient training so they could then turn around and raise their own children to function independently and separately from their family's constant supervision.

Despite the experiences of the past and the current challenges that are before us, with proper training and consistent parenting, the next generation can receive a better legacy. We have an opportunity and obligation to properly teach all children, whether in our homes, at school, or in other settings. First, we must be appropriately disciplined ourselves. Second, we must model an optimistic lifestyle for our family members that includes a strong work ethic, consistency, honesty, kindness, service, patience, and taking responsibility.

Even as we want to understand the *why* and *what* of childrearing, sometimes the best methods are learning the *hows* of parenting. There are significant skills that when taught, practiced, and modeled will help children of any age improve their ability to be contributing individuals. These specific skills will magnify with time until they bloom freely in adulthood and children mature into useful, dependable, and contributing members of their workplaces, homes, and communities.

Parents have fewer than twenty years to initially influence a child. Much of this influential nurturing takes place in the very early years, and the rest is received or rejected as children gain momentum, moods, and muscle to their personalities.

Of course there will be continued nurturing of these same children as they approach adulthood and even move into their mature years, but *now* is the time to make the biggest difference in your children's lives. Now is the time to initiate change and model a better way.

Because I understand that not all children have two parents in the home, when I speak of parents I am addressing the primary mentor(s) in a child's life. This might be parents, stepparents, grandparents, foster parents, guardians, older siblings, aunts, uncles, Church leaders and teachers, or any other significant adult in the child's life. Whoever you are and whatever title you carry, you can be a noteworthy force for good any and every time you mentor a child.

If you will carefully read and put into practice the principles discussed in this book, you will be well on your way to more successful parenting and having more responsible children.

PART ONE: *Prepare to Parent Better*

CHAPTER ONE

Prepare to Train

You will give your children many gifts during the twenty years or so of your direct stewardship over them, but an important part of that stewardship will be your opportunity to properly train them how to act, work, and strive for personal life skills. For the purposes of this book, I am differentiating "training" from "teaching." "Training" means to teach children how to do projects, jobs, and chores. "Teaching" relates to instruction on how to respond to different challenges and difficulties in life with morality and integrity.

To be effective, you must first be what you want your children to be. You cannot ignore the small imperfections in your personality. Eventually, the child will discover those inconsistencies and, if you are not true to what you are trying to train your children to be, they will feel betrayed and have difficulty continuing to trust you. That is one reason parents should not lie when they don't want to answer a phone call, should not speed when they are in a hurry, and should not steal or cheat even to the smallest degree. For it is in the small things that our characters are shaped. You cannot expect to have long-term influence on your children if you try to train them to act one way while your example illustrates a different behavior.

One of the sure ways to begin this personal preparation for training is to declutter your life. Decluttering means not only ridding yourself of unnecessary possessions and cleaning up your personal space but also discarding any habits that will make you less than an able teacher. It means moving yourself to a place where you can confidently train your children in how to act, knowing they will see those same actions modeled in your daily walk.

You don't need to be perfect, but your children initially will think you are, so you'll want to be as good a mentor as you can. They will want to see your bed made if you are teaching them to make their own. They need to see you put your dishes in the dishwasher after a meal if you want them to do so.

Effective parents know that routines and rituals are very useful to childrearing. Younger children especially like to know that you can be depended upon. For example, can they count on a bedtime story every night as you tuck them into bed? Can they look forward to family prayer every morning before the day's activities? Do they know they have chores that need to be accomplished every afternoon before dinnertime?

Finally, remember that you must be an interesting person to retain their interest. You want your children to always be amenable to tutoring. As you prepare to train your children how to work, be on the lookout for something to share that they will find intriguing. Be willing to share any and all housekeeping or gardening skills, tips, or time-saving hints that you know with them. An interesting question can always be, "Mitch, do you know how to . . . ? No? Well, let me show you how and then you can try it yourself."

As you prepare to train, you need to keep in mind several key rules.

First, structure your training. Follow the same pattern each time: you talk, you show, you allow children to try, you instruct some more, you determine if they are ready to do it again, you let them try, you correct, and so on. This time of training cannot be haphazard or casual. It must be intentional and more formal to be recognized by your children as important. Children must feel your love, your desire to share, and your knowledge to help them learn the skill. They must realize that you can be trusted to show them the best way to do a job, all the way to the finish.

Second, identify the specific procedures you want your children to follow. You have your own particular methods and skills that you want to pass on. Certainly there are many ways to do even the simplest task, but during the initial stages of training, it is important that you direct your children to do it the same way over and over again. This will improve their ability to do the job well, to do it faster, and to do it until it becomes comfortably routine. Then they can explore different and possibly better, more creative ways to approach the job.

Third, time your training, both in length and when it will happen, to get the most out of it. A tired child is not a willing child. A hungry child is not a cooperative child. An unhappy child is not an accommodating child. However, a curious child will learn quickly. An energetic child will receive instruction with great interest, and a child who feels loved and needed will desire to please.

The season for children to want to duplicate, to learn tasks, and to model their parents' behavior is very short and quite early in their lives. Whenever possible, let them "help" when they are small and underfoot so they will continue to be willing to help when they are older and have other areas of interest.

For example, one wise father wanted his youngest son to participate with him when they did yard work together. He made a wooden lawn mower for his son to push around the lawn while he used the real lawn mower. When the child grew tall enough to reach up and hold the real mower's handle, his father let him push it to the starting place all by himself before the father started it up and the son returned to his wooden mower. Eventually, the son became more and more involved in yard work until he took over the lawn mowing while his father worked on trimming, edging, and other detail work. Finally, the son took over all the yard responsibilities completely when the father began to travel for his occupation. The father realized that the season for training had to begin early, and he was rewarded with a son who was competent, capable, and well trained.

Fourth, give your children perspective as you train them to work. They need to know from your own mouth how essential they are to the success of your family and how important it is to you that they are learning to do as you do. They need to hear that you enjoy being with them and showing them how things are done right and also that you look forward to working with them again and again. Let them know you are willing to train them with every skill you know. Help them see that small skills learned now will help them be able to learn more complex skills as they mature. Talk about professional surveying when you lay a line of string for planting seeds in the garden, discuss building a real house when you patch a hall wall, and help them envision supporting their own family while you repair the flat bicycle tire together. Help them see that whatever they learn now will be useful for other seasons in their lives.

CHAPTER TWO

Prepare to Show

Parenting is a show-and-tell adventure. Almost everything that you know, your attitudes about life, and your current talents can be passed on to your children. Much of who you are they will pick up just by being around you. And sometimes it will astound and shame you to see how completely they have learned just by being in your presence. Having said that, it is important to show children the proper method you want them to use for every skill they will learn. Yes, they will learn other ways to do things and, yes, you and your spouse might even have two different methods, and the children will benefit from learning both. However, you must show them if you are to have them learn well.

Let's take the simple example of training children how to put a coat on a hanger. Show them the method of holding the nape of the neck of the coat next to the hanger, how to slip the coat over each end of the hanger, and how to carefully hold the coat and hanger with one hand while separating and pushing aside clothes in their closet with the other hand to accommodate the insertion of the coat. This is a simple skill (and one made easier if children can easily reach the rod), but it is one that is best shown for it to be learned right. Otherwise, you will find that children will tend to dump their coats on the floor, leave them around the house, and even hide them in unusual places, mostly because they were not shown the right way to hang up a coat and then encouraged to do so every time they took off their coats.

In some respects "showing" often precedes and always accompanies the practice of "training." For example, long before children will actually mop the floor themselves they might be sitting in the high chair eating Cheerios while you mop the floor. As they watch you work, they are being shown the method for mopping the kitchen floor. You can also model your method with the addition of an explanation.

"Watch how I move the chairs aside, sweep up the floor with the broom and dust pan, wet the mop pad, and begin to mop first in the corner farthest from the sink. Now I work my way back to the sink so I can clean the mop head from time to time as I mop."

Showing your child the methods by which you work and monologuing as you go is a great way to prepare a child for the excitement of participation, especially if you continue your conversation by saying:

"Your brother and sister both know how to mop a floor too. They do it for our family as part of their chores. When you are old enough to go to school, I will train you how to mop a floor, and then you can take turns with them."

Some might say that such conversations with a toddler are useless and fly right over their little heads, but my experience has been exactly the opposite. Children are always learning. They observe and learn with every interaction they have with you. Of course, sometimes you will be too preoccupied to pay any attention to them when you mop and will be glad they are quietly eating their Cheerios and leaving you to your thoughts. However, as parents regularly take advantage of opportuni-ties to show children how to do a skill, how to complete a task, and what methods they use to get from here to there in a chore, they are preparing their children to do the same in later years.

CHAPTER THREE

Prepare to Nurture

To have extraordinary children you must first be an extraordinary parent. No one else needs to know that you are extraordinary, and you will have many years of training ahead of you to understand parenting as a whole, but still, you must be extraordinary *now* to begin the journey. And because all human beings are extraordinary, you are already there. It is sometimes easy to forget that being extraordinary mostly means looking after what is most important first and then taking care of the rest of life afterward. In other words, if you are a parent or are going to be a parent, it is time to learn and train for the important, significant, and absolutely vital skills of parenting.

Parenting takes time, lots of it. It also takes energy, more than you will sometimes possess. And it takes a lot of patience, too. But it is one of the most fulfilling of any and all the pursuits of life because you have been entrusted by God to raise one or more of His holy children.

Children become like those whom they live with, those whom they know the most personally, and especially those who care about them. You are doing something wonderful with your life when you decide to parent. You can pass on to your children the extraordinary parts of your soul, the experiences that have ennobled you, and the beliefs and values that shape your heart for their experimentation, exploration, and eventual acceptance.

But you must prepare to be a better parent. The preparation will continue the entire time you have children in the home and should continue when they are grown and gone—you can always be evolving into the best parent you want to be. Your influence continues when they have matured and left the nest to live their own lives; it just changes. But it is still there. To be an extraordinary parent means to learn better how to nurture, train, discipline, show, and teach your children, whatever their ages and maturity.

However fulfilling parenting is, it is also sometimes a frustrating occupation. It will take all you have to understand today's children, only to wake tomorrow to new creatures with emerging attitudes, frightening tendencies, and unexpected responses to the difficulties of the new day.

One of the first skills of successful parenting is to understand the deep need all children have to be valued, respected, and loved. I call this the desire to be *nurtured*. When they are infants and young children, they want to be held close, picked up immediately when they call, and have your attention constantly. They just want to be wanted. If you respond with love and generosity, you will teach the children in your care that the world is a safe place and that you can be trusted to care for them.

A second important preparation skill is being able to respond to the world with gentleness. If you want your older children to touch softly, hold gently, and move slowly in fragile environments, you will need to practice this skill yourself, whether you are the father or the mother. Nurturing implies a gentle touch. It includes the skill of speaking with a calm, peaceful voice and avoiding the natural tendency to enforce your will by the superiority of your size and the volume of your call. Influencing through nurturing implies wisdom, kindness, and the highest level of reliability.

Third, children, of all creatures, need encouragement. They need a coach who is also their cheerleader. They need someone who will love them when they err, hug them when they have messed up, and support them when they make mistakes. This capacity to encourage can be enlarged day to day in your anticipation of parenting by encouraging those within your current circle of life. The newspaper boy needs to know that you appreciate his accurate throw, the elderly neighbor needs a compliment on his beautiful flower bed, and the distracted clerk at the grocery store needs a positive comment about how she packs the produce in your bag. Looking for the good in all who surround your days will naturally increase your capacity to encourage your children. Looking to nurture others now will help you be a better parent in the future.

CHAPTER FOUR

Prepare to Teach

Even as you show your children how to do many things during the first years of their lives, you also teach them about the values and character traits that you hold dear. In this book, when I speak of teaching children, it will be about their moral and character maturation. When I speak of training, it will be to focus on the mental and physical skills important to children's development.

For example, when you model positive skills of social interaction for your children, you teach them sensitivity to others' feelings, how to handle public situations with grace, and how to find courage to stand for the right. It is through teaching that you are provided with your greatest opportunity to influence other valuable human beings to do good.

So the questions arise, what kind of people do you want to raise and how do you move to that place yourself? Do you treat others with respect in public and private? Do you use deference when attacked verbally by others? Do you have self-control and abstain from all substances that you wouldn't want your children to use? Does your home reflect the high standards you hope your children will emulate? If not, it is time to improve your environment, change unappealing aspects of your own personality, and develop your interactions to a level of acceptability to you. Your children will, most likely, become what you teach, and you teach primarily by example and precept. Will your example reflect the best of what you want them to be?

Teaching children must be done with the understanding that they will need the chance to explore the new concepts you have taught. They will need encouragement, they will need patience when they fail, and they will need praise for every worthy effort they make. They also need to be shown the process of how to move from problems to solutions. Many times, when a problem presents itself in your life, you may become frozen in "whine mode." This means you feel incapacitated to resolve the challenge and so find relief in complaining. As you prepare to parent, develop the habit of seeing a problem when it arises, looking at it squarely, and searching for a solution to the difficulty. Begin to move from problems to solutions in your own life wherever possible. This will make it easier to teach this skill to your children.

When you find yourself complaining, realize you are frozen with inaction and have reverted to whining. If you whine, your children will also whine. How much easier it is to make significant changes now in your own reactions to life's many challenges. If you begin now to move from problems to solutions, looking for answers and resolutions, you will find that this habit will easily be modeled and transferred to your children through opportune teaching moments. Become a problem solver to be a better, more effective parent. Prepare now to become a great teacher, both by instruction and your own example.

After you have looked inward, have done an assessment, and are working on changes and improvement, you are ready for the adventure of training and teaching your children to be the best, most extraordinary adults they are capable of becoming!

PART TWO: *Train Them*

CHAPTER FIVE

A Master Plan

This chapter is not intended to overwhelm or frustrate you. There are a lot of chores that children need to learn how to do, but they don't need to be taught them all at once, nor should they be assigned to do all of them every day or every week. Teaching your children various chores should be spread out throughout their growing-up years so that they maintain a good balance of school, church, play, personal time, and home chore activities.

Household Chores

There are three categories of household and yard chores that should be taught to children: personal skills, daily chores, and complex jobs.

Personal Skills. When children are very young, they can be taught simple tasks to groom themselves, make their bedrooms neat, and help their parents with everyday routines. These activities might include chores that make the home more orderly, such as making their beds, putting their dirty clothes in the laundry basket, and combing their hair. These jobs are usually taught to children during the first six years of their lives. Since these jobs usually need attending to at least once a day, if not more often, it is easy to get into a simple routine of doing chores. Some jobs will happen only occasionally during the week, as needed. The goal here is to teach the methods for doing a chore, help the children acquire skills to follow a routine, and then provide them opportunities to use the tools you have given them to finish their work.

"John, here are three new combs: red, blue, and green. Which one would you like to be your comb? Green? That is great. Up to now Dad or I have combed your hair. Today begins something new. You get to comb your hair all by yourself. You get to use this 'Johnny Green' comb (see the combination of your first name and the color of the comb?) every morning to make your hair look neat after you have bathed. I know you have watched as your dad or I have combed your hair. Now I'll describe to you how to comb your hair, then you can practice, and then we'll get out a mirror and see if you like how you look, both in front and in back. Pretty soon you will be combing your hair without even being reminded."

Daily Chores. The second category of jobs children should learn are those that involve regular cleaning. These are usually given to children who have begun their formal schooling, primarily during the ages of six to twelve. These jobs might include sweeping the kitchen floor, dusting the front room, and cleaning the bathroom. More and more difficult jobs are given to children ages six to twelve as they mature, become strong enough for more complex work, and can understand that while some jobs are done every day others are done only occasionally during the week. For example, vacuuming the family room might be done Monday, Wednesday, and Friday, and the bathrooms might be cleaned on Saturday.

"Kaitlyn, here is a pair of small plastic gloves just for you, so you can clean the bathroom basin. I also bought you a small tote for storing your bathroom cleaning supplies. It really means a lot to me that you can clean the sink, wipe down the counters, and dust the top of the toilet on Saturdays. Thanks."

Complex Jobs. The third category of jobs includes those where scrubbing is required. Not only will the maturing youth, now ages twelve to eighteen, need to remember to do the jobs occasionally during the week, month, or year, but they will also be trusted with even more complex activities like taking the garbage to the street on Friday mornings, mowing the lawn on Saturdays, and cleaning the blinds twice a year.

"Michael, I'm glad you've agreed to take the garbage to the street each week. I know it will be hard at first to remember on your own to do it without being reminded, but I trust you will find a system that will get that garbage can out on Fridays before you leave for school. What are your ideas? Oh, you have a computer program that can remind you? Great."

Now that household jobs have been categorized into three general areas (personal skills, daily chores, and complex jobs), let's focus on three additional terms: tools, systems, and routines.

Tools. Children who are given their own set of tools are more likely to feel that they "own" the jobs they are given. I like to give children the tools appropriate to their responsibilities, let them label and decorate them as they desire, and let them have their own cleaning tote. Depending on their responsibilities, their tote might include plastic gloves, a dusting mitt, cleaning cloths, and an apron.

Systems. Once their tools have been acquired, labeled, and have a "home," it is useful to train your children modeling the exact method you would like them to use to complete the job.

"Sam, when we mop the kitchen floor, here is what we do. First, we move all the chairs onto the family room rug and sweep the floor. Next we get out the mop and dip it in warm, soapy water. Then we mop back and forth all around the kitchen counters and table. The last thing we do is mop past the back door and back to the kitchen sink again. This puts us right where we need to be to wring out the mop."

Routines. Finally, you will need to establish definite routines so those in your family can anticipate the frequency of jobs.

"Yes, Micah, we make our beds every day, but we change the sheets only once a week, and we turn the mattresses only once a year. You are right; we turn your mattresses on the day before your birthday. Wow, you have a good memory!"

Setting Up a Master Plan

As you contemplate the training of your children, what skills you will help them obtain, and your long-term desires for their work ethic, it is useful to set up a *Training Children to Work Master Plan*. This plan can serve as the foundation for the training of your family members and make your long-term goals possible by defining the smaller, more specific skills you desire your children to obtain. It will also allow you to decide at what ages you will introduce different skills to them.

In the many years of personal organization I have done, I have discovered that a simple 3" x 5" index card system is the most successful, flexible tool for setting up a Training Children to Work Master Plan. Index cards have a great advantage because they can be moved around on a table when you are working with your children. The cards are tangible evidence of the children's progress if you write a handwritten note on the back of the card regarding their success. Also add the date when your children "pass" their first inspection and conquer the skill. These cards will also serve as a reminder to you about past events. For example, you might say:

> "Ryan, your older brother successfully learned to clean the toilet when he was your age. That would have been seven years ago. See, here are my notes when he passed off the first inspection. Wow, Ryan, I think you are ready to learn how to clean toilets too!"

Master Plan Dividers

The Training Children to Work Master Plan index cards are prepared by the parents and stored in a sturdy index card box with twelve dividers labeled:

- Daily
- Monday
- Tuesday
- Wednesday
- Thursday
- Friday
- Saturday
- Sunday
- 2–6 Years
- 6–12 Years
- 12–18 Years
- Extra Cards

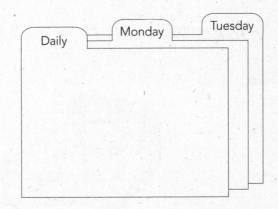

The *Daily* and *Monday–Sunday* dividers are for jobs the children are currently doing. These are the reminders to parents for what needs to be done by each child each day. The *2–6 Years*, *6–12 Years*, and *12–18 Years* dividers are where the skill cards not being currently used are kept for future use. The *Extra Cards* divider is where spare, blank cards are kept.

Master Plan Index Card Setup

The individual Training Children to Work Master Plan 3" x 5" index cards are prepared by the parents or other adults in the family. (See www.houseoforder.com for products you can purchase.) The job you desire to train your children to do is listed in the upper left-hand corner of the index card and the frequency of the chore is listed in the upper right-hand corner. Especially for younger children, the addition of a simple picture or some clip art helps them understand what the card means even before they can read.

For example, a card for making beds might be prepared as shown below:

In a hypothetical home with a living room, family room, kitchen, bathroom, child's room, and baby's room (with master bedroom and master bathroom jobs being retained by the adults of the home), index cards would be made for cleaning each room. Practical skill cards would also be made for additional home management jobs, as would cards for self-education and enrichment.

Master Plan Cards—Ages 2–6

For children ages two to six, the Master Plan cards might read:

Ages 2–6 Daily Morning Chores

- ❐ Wash my face—Daily
- ❐ Get dressed—Daily
- ❐ Put on my shoes—Daily
- ❐ Tie my shoelaces—Daily
- ❐ Comb my hair—Daily
- ❐ Say my personal prayers—Daily
- ❐ Read my scriptures—Daily
- ❐ Eat breakfast—Daily
- ❐ Clear my dishes from the table after meals—Daily
- ❐ Brush my teeth after meals—Daily
- ❐ Hang up my clothes—Daily
- ❐ Straighten my books—Daily
- ❐ Tidy my bedroom—Daily
- ❐ Serve someone—Daily (an important skill to introduce early in a child's life)

Ages 2–6 School Work Skills

☐ Learn my first, middle, and last names

☐ Write my first, middle, and last names

☐ Learn my birthdate

☐ Write my birthdate

☐ Learn the numbers 1–10

☐ Write the numbers 1–10

☐ Learn my phone number (including area code)

☐ Write my phone number

☐ Learn my address

☐ Write my address

☐ Learn my colors

Ages 2–6 Household Chores

☐ Put my toys away before lunch—Daily

☐ Put my toys away before dinner—Daily

☐ Push the table chairs in after meals—Daily

Ages 2–6 Occasional Chores

☐ Put my pajamas in the dirty clothes basket—Friday

☐ Put my laundry away—Monday, Wednesday, Friday

☐ Empty my bedroom wastebasket—The day before trash is picked up

Tiny Tot Chore Charts

As you decide how to help preschool-age children "own" their jobs, you might consider the following. Small children readily respond to bright visual cues and enjoy having their own set of chore cards or charts to keep and use. After you have decided what chores you would like your children to do and the skills you would like them to learn, you could print these up on sturdy cardstock and have them laminated and punched in the upper left-hand corner. A binder ring can then be used to hold the cards together. As each chore is taught to the young children, they can graduate to having more cards as they learn the skills and practice them. This allows for progress to be marked, for the children to have increasing independence, and for parents to reward the children with more cards.

Below is a possible simple formatting for such cards, using larger letters and simple artwork. (See www.houseoforder.com for products you can purchase.)

Master Plan Cards—Ages 6–12

For children ages six to twelve the Training Children to Work Master Plan cards might read as illustrated below. These chores are best explained, demonstrated, and practiced initially by children during summer (or vacation) months, with a limited number of chores continued during the school months. The days of the week attached to these chores on these sample Master Plan cards show how to spread the work over a week's time and are meant only for use as examples. Of course, when you prepare your own, you will change the frequency and specific days these chores are done according to your preference and schedule. Some of the chores are complicated enough that detailed instructions might be included on your Master Plan cards for easy reference during training (see the sample bathroom cleaning card below). Again, the title of the job goes in the upper left-hand corner of the index card and the frequency of the job performance goes in the upper right-hand corner of the index card, with detailed instructions written out as needed.

You will note that most of the skills are learned between the ages of six and twelve. Most teenagers begin to leave the home more frequently for outside jobs and thus much of their training should be in place before they turn twelve.

Clean bathroom sink   Tuesday

- Wipe mirror and counter.
- Scrub sink, soap holder, and toothbrush holder.
- Shine taps.

Ages 6–12 Morning Summertime Chores

- ❏ Empty dishes from dishwasher—Daily
- ❏ Set breakfast table—Daily
- ❏ Help fix breakfast—Daily
- ❏ Clean up from breakfast—Daily
- ❏ Tidy living room—Daily
- ❏ Tidy family room—Daily
- ❏ Tidy bathroom—Daily
- ❏ Tidy kitchen—Daily
- ❏ Tidy office or den—Daily
- ❏ Tidy baby's room—Daily
- ❏ Feed and water pet—Daily

Lunchtime during summer months is an excellent time to begin training your children how to cook. Depending on the number of children you have and their interests, you might consider letting them have one day each week when they prepare lunch, set the table, serve the meal, and clean up (with your help, of course). If this idea suits you, it is useful at the beginning of summer to print out three months' worth of monthly calendars and to also make a list of possible meals you would like to train them to prepare. Then sit down with your children and let them choose from this previously prepared menu what meals they would like to prepare on their days to cook. As they choose, write their choices on the three monthly calendars. This adds variety to your summer lunches and helps your children learn different kinds of cooking skills. A simple monthly summer lunch menu example follows for a family of four children learning the rudiments of making sandwiches, preparing eggs, and cooking muffins.

Week	Monday Timothy	Wednesday Katie	Thursday Christopher	Friday Elizabeth
1	ham & cheese	tomato soup	peanut butter	fried eggs
2	tomato soup	scrambled eggs	corn muffins	noodle soup
3	boiled eggs	French muffins	tomato soup	peanut butter
4	egg muffins	tacos	pigs in blanket	tomato soup
5	tuna fish	ham & cheese	fried eggs	scrambled eggs
6	fried eggs	tuna fish	ham & cheese	French muffins
7	noodle soup	corn muffins	tuna fish	egg muffins
8	tacos	boiled eggs	egg muffins	tuna fish
9	pigs in blanket	egg muffins	boiled eggs	ham & cheese
10	corn muffins	ham & cheese	tacos	pigs in blanket
11	scrambled eggs	fried eggs	noodle soup	tacos
12	French muffins	pigs in blanket	corn muffins	boiled eggs

Ages 6–12 Lunch Summertime Chores

☐ Empty dishwasher of breakfast dishes—My Day

☐ Set table for lunch—My Day

☐ Help fix lunch—My Day

☐ Help clean up after lunch—My Day

Ages 6–12 Dinner Summertime Chores

☐ Empty dishwasher of lunch dishes—My Day

☐ Set table for dinner—My Day

☐ Help fix dinner—My Day

☐ Help clean up after dinner—My Day

Ages 6–12 Personal Summertime Skills

- ❐ Do my exercises (an especially important skill for children who struggle with their weight)—Daily

- ❐ Practice my musical instrument—Daily

- ❐ Read my book(s)—Daily

- ❐ Review my addition facts—Daily (age appropriate)

- ❐ Review my subtraction facts—Daily (age appropriate)

- ❐ Review my multiplication facts—Daily (age appropriate)

- ❐ Review my division facts—Daily (age appropriate)

- ❐ Practice using a calculator—Daily

- ❐ Practice typing on the computer—Daily

Ages 6–12 Household Summertime Chores—Monday, Wednesday, Friday

- ❐ Clean the bathroom toilet—Monday, Wednesday, Friday

- ❐ Sweep kitchen floor—Monday, Wednesday, Friday

- ❐ Vacuum living room—Monday, Wednesday, Friday

- ❐ Vacuum family room—Monday, Wednesday, Friday

- ❐ Collect dirty clothes—Monday, Wednesday, Friday

- ❐ Sort laundry: lights, mediums, darks, hand wash—Monday, Wednesday, Friday

- ❐ Fold my clean laundry—Monday, Wednesday, Friday

- ❐ Put my laundry away—Monday, Wednesday, Friday

Ages 6–12 Household Summertime Chores—Tuesday, Thursday

- ❏ Vacuum hall—Tuesday, Thursday
- ❏ Vacuum my bedroom—Tuesday, Thursday

Ages 6–12 Household Summertime Chores—Tuesday

- ❏ Collect bath towels for washing—Tuesday
- ❏ Return clean towels to their racks—Tuesday
- ❏ Clean bathroom sink: Wipe mirror and counter. Scrub sink, soap holder, and toothbrush holder. Shine taps—Tuesday
- ❏ Clean bathtub: Scrub bathtub, soap holder, and tub surround. Shine bathtub taps—Tuesday
- ❏ Clean bathroom floor: Shake bathroom rug, sweep and mop bathroom floor. Return rug to floor and straighten—Tuesday
- ❏ Clean toilet: Wipe down top, tank, lid (outside and in), seat (outside and in), outside, rim, bowl. Flush. Dry everything with a clean cloth—Tuesday

Ages 6–12 Household Summertime Chores—Wednesday

- ❏ Dust living room: Dust windowsills, tables, lamps, piano, and fireplace screen—Wednesday
- ❏ Dust family room: Dust windowsills, tables, lamps, TV, stereo, bookcases—Wednesday
- ❏ Dust my bedroom: Dust windowsill, chest of drawers, desk, chair, lamp, and end table—Wednesday
- ❏ Dust baby's bedroom: Dust windowsill, chest of drawers, crib, chair, lamp, rocker, and end table—Wednesday

Ages 6–12 Household Summertime Chores—Thursday

- ❏ Clean kitchen floor: Move chairs, sweep floor, mop floor, put chairs back—Thursday
- ❏ Clean kitchen stove: Wipe top, dials, burner drip pans, oven door, and oven drawer—Thursday
- ❏ Clean microwave: Wipe front, top, and insides—Thursday
- ❏ Clean kitchen counters—Thursday
- ❏ Clean kitchen table: Wipe table, chair backs and fronts, chair seats—Thursday
- ❏ Clean kitchen refrigerator: Wipe front, sides, and insides —Thursday
- ❏ Clean kitchen sink: Scrub out bowl, rinse well, dry and shine sink, clean and shine taps—Thursday

Ages 6–12 Household Summertime Chores—Friday

- ❏ Help with mending—Friday
- ❏ Help with ironing—Friday
- ❏ Change my bed: Take dirty sheets and pillowcase off my bed and put in laundry room—Friday
- ❏ Make up my bed with clean sheets and pillowcase—Friday
- ❏ Water the houseplants—Friday

Ages 6–12 Household Summertime Chores—Saturday

- ❏ Sweep front porch—Saturday
- ❏ Sweep back porch—Saturday

Ages 6–12 Household Summertime Chores—Sunday

- ❏ Write in my journal—Sunday

❏ Write and mail thank-you notes, letters, and e-mails (to my grandparents, an older sibling, someone serving in the military, a friend, a missionary, or someone who is sick)—Sunday

❏ Pay my tithing and fast offerings—Sunday

Master Plan Cards—Ages 12–18

For youth ages twelve to eighteen the Master Plan cards might read as follows. These new, more complex chores are in addition to the ones young people will continue to practice as they do chores they have been taught since they were young. Again, these chores are explained, demonstrated, and practiced initially by youth during summer months, with a limited number of chores continued during the school year. The days of the week attached to these chores on the Master Plan cards could be determined by the schedule of the teenager and other members of the household. These are examples only and will change according to your preference and schedules when you prepare your own. Some of the chores are complicated enough that detailed instructions might be included on your Master Plan cards for easy reference during training (as seen in the sample bathroom cleaning card on page 30).

Remember, it is never too late to begin this training, no matter the ages of your children. Just start with the beginning skills, work with your children until you feel they are well-trained in those chores, and then supervise them for continual support. Make sure the two-to-six-year-old skills are taught first, then the six-to-twelve-year-old skills, and finally the twelve-to-eighteen-year-old skills.

Ages 12–18 Summertime Chores

❏ Do my laundry: Collect the clothes, wash them, dry them, fold or hang them, put them away—Every week on _____

- ☐ Change my bed linen: Take off sheets and pillowcase, wash and dry them, remake my bed—Every week on _____

- ☐ Prepare weekly menu—Every week on _____

- ☐ Prepare weekly grocery list—Every week on _____

- ☐ Do grocery shopping—Every week on _____ (usually for teenagers who can drive)

- ☐ Put groceries away—Every week on _____

- ☐ Mow lawn—Every week on _____

- ☐ Trim lawn—Every week on _____

- ☐ Weed flower gardens—Every week on _____

- ☐ Weed vegetable garden—Every week on _____

- ☐ Clean and vacuum inside family vehicle—Every week on _____

- ☐ Wash family vehicle—Every week on _____

- ☐ Pay my tithing and fast offering—Monthly

- ☐ Update and balance my budget—Monthly

A final note: some parents keep their Master Plan cards as a resource set from which to determine who will do what during the upcoming season and have their children make their own individual index cards detailing their jobs each season. In this case, the children will also need a set of *Daily, Monday–Sunday,* and *Extra Cards* dividers and a personal index box to keep their cards neat.

Master Plan cards are also useful as a reference when making charts detailing children's jobs for the summer. Parents can add stickers or other visuals to monitor progress and help the children set goals.

Master Plan cards may also be duplicated so that children have their own complete sets of index cards to use as they mature. The way you implement the use of the Master Plan cards is not as important as making sure they are prepared, maintained, and used year after year to help you in raising hardworking, competent children.

Cleaning Tools

As you prepare to train your children, it is useful to let them have their own personal cleaning tool kit. Other tools, such as the vacuum and each bathroom's toilet brush, will be stored in a consistent place, but consider supplying your children with their own labeled plastic gloves, a tote for sponges, rags, and scrub brushes, and a pocketed apron to store found items in as they move from room to room. This personal ownership of tools helps children feel more invested in cleaning the house, too.

Standards Charts

After the Training Children to Work Master Plan cards are prepared, parents would do well to identify the standards for the different household jobs for which they will be training their children. This will encourage consistency in the work and give a standard measurement for examining the completed chore.

On the pages that follow are some examples of standards for both "Fast Clean" (when there is little time or less cleaning is needed) and "Deep Clean" (when there is more time or greater cleaning is needed) of various rooms in the house. As you will easily see, having such standards eliminates confusion, focuses energy, and allows all involved family members to know when a job has been correctly and completely finished. The Standards charts can be duplicated, laminated, and posted in the appropriate areas of your home.

After laminating, a white-board marker can be used to check off each task as it is completed. (See www.houseoforder.com for premade sets of laminated Standards charts.)

Other household jobs, such as washing a car, also need an identifiable standard of acceptance. Of course, over time the Standards charts will not be used as much as they will be in the beginning. But they are extremely useful during the training period. For all jobs you intend to teach your family members, seriously consider taking the time now to establish your standards, write them down, and make them available to your children in a printed form.

Fast Clean of Living Room and Family Room

☐ Put away all items in room:

- Put in their rightful place in room OR
- Put in plastic transfer container (for things that belong in other rooms)

☐ Straighten cushions on couches and chairs, items on end tables, magazines, books, and all other items

☐ Open blinds or curtains

☐ Look around once more and make sure it looks good enough for company!

☐ Put away items in plastic transfer container where they belong

Deep Clean of Living Room and Family Room

- ☐ Put away all items in room:
  - Put in their rightful place in room OR
  - Put in plastic transfer container (for things that belong in other rooms)

- ☐ Straighten cushions on couches and chairs, items on end tables, magazines, books and all other items.

- ☐ Open blinds or curtains

- ☐ Dust windowsills, tables, lamp bases and lamp shades, picture frames, window blinds, mantels, figurines, and bookshelves

- ☐ Dry mop floor, shake rugs, and vacuum carpet

- ☐ Look around once more and make sure it looks really clean!

- ☐ Put away items in plastic transfer container where they belong

Fast Clean of Kitchen

☐ Clear dishes and other items from table and counters:

- Put dishes in dishwasher OR in a sink full of warm, soapy water

- Put items away where they belong in kitchen

- Put other items in plastic transfer container (for things that belong in other rooms)

☐ Put trash in wastebasket

☐ Wipe table and counters

☐ Push chairs in around table

☐ Put centerpiece on center of table

☐ Straighten rugs

☐ Look around once more and make sure it looks nice!

☐ Put away items in plastic transfer container where they belong

Deep Clean of Kitchen

☐ Clear dishes and other items from table and counters:

- Put dishes in dishwasher or in sink full of warm, soapy water
- Put other items away or in plastic transfer container (for things that belong in other rooms)

☐ Wipe table and counters

☐ Clean kitchen chairs—wipe chair backs, fronts, seats, and legs

☐ Clean microwave—inside and out

☐ Clean stove—wipe down exterior, dials, burner drip pans

☐ Clean refrigerator—wipe front, sides, insides, and top

☐ Shake rugs and leave outside kitchen door

☐ Move chairs, sweep and mop kitchen floor

☐ Clean mop and put away

☐ Push chairs in around table

☐ Return rugs and straighten

☐ Put centerpiece on center of table

☐ Empty wastebasket

☐ Look around and make sure it looks really clean!

☐ Put away items in plastic transfer container where they belong

Fast Clean of Bathroom

- ☐ Put all dirty clothes in laundry basket

- ☐ Straighten towels and rugs

- ☐ Put away all items in bathroom:

  - Put in their rightful place in bathroom OR

  - Put in plastic transfer container (for things that belong in other rooms)

- ☐ Close vanity doors, drawers, and cupboard doors

- ☐ Wipe down counters, clean sinks, and shine taps with cleaning cloths

- ☐ Clean toilet rim between seat and bowl

- ☐ Put down toilet lid and flush

- ☐ Put cleaning cloths in laundry basket

- ☐ Confirm there is enough toilet paper on roll

- ☐ Look around and make sure it looks great!

- ☐ Put away items in plastic transfer container where they belong

Deep Clean of Bathroom

- ☐ Put all dirty clothes in laundry basket
- ☐ Straighten towels
- ☐ Shake rugs and leave outside bathroom door
- ☐ Put away all items in bathroom:
  - Put in their rightful place in bathroom OR
  - Put in plastic transfer container (for things that belong in other rooms)
- ☐ Close vanity doors, drawers, and cupboard doors
- ☐ Clean mirrors with cleaning cloth
- ☐ Wipe down counters, clean sinks, and shine taps
- ☐ Scrub and rinse bathtub and shower enclosure and taps
- ☐ Shine bathtub and shower taps
- ☐ Sweep and mop floor
- ☐ Clean toilet tank top, lid, seat (outside and in), exterior, rim, and bowl. Flush.
- ☐ Wipe outside of toilet with dry cleaning cloth and put down toilet lid
- ☐ Confirm there is enough toilet paper on roll
- ☐ Return rugs to bathroom and straighten
- ☐ Empty wastebasket
- ☐ Look around once more and make sure it looks really clean!
- ☐ Put away items in plastic transfer container where they belong

Fast Clean of Bedroom

- ☐ Put away all items in bedroom:
    - Put in their rightful place in bedroom OR
    - Put in plastic transfer container (for things that belong in other rooms)
- ☐ Straighten desk items, books, and toys
- ☐ Clean off top of chest of drawers
- ☐ Put dirty clothes in laundry basket
- ☐ Make bed
- ☐ Open curtains
- ☐ Close closet doors and drawers
- ☐ Put trash in wastebasket
- ☐ Look around once more and make sure it looks great!
- ☐ Put away items in plastic transfer container where they belong

Deep Clean of Bedroom

- ☐ Put away all items in bedroom:

  - Put in their rightful place in bedroom OR

  - Put in plastic transfer container (for things that belong in other rooms)

- ☐ Straighten desk items, books, and toys

- ☐ Put dirty clothes in laundry basket

- ☐ Clean off top of chest of drawers

- ☐ Make bed

- ☐ Open curtains

- ☐ Close closet doors and drawers

- ☐ Dust bedroom—windowsill, chest of drawers, desk, chair, lamp, and all other surfaces

- ☐ Dry mop floor or vacuum carpet

- ☐ Empty wastebasket

- ☐ Look around once more and make sure it looks really clean!

- ☐ Put away items in plastic transfer container where they belong

CHAPTER SIX

Obedience Is First, Honesty Is Second, and Their Bedroom Is Third

With the Training Children to Work Master Plan in place, it is time to focus on the foundations of this training. We'll start first with obedience.

Obedience

There are so many aspects of teaching children how they should conduct themselves. All children benefit when they are taught to be obedient. When children learn to obey willingly, they are on their way to self-discipline.

Do your children come to you the first time you ask? Do they obey when your voice is still soft and kind? Or have they learned they can wait until your voice reaches a certain volume and a specific pitch before they know you are really serious? Do you often resort to the "one, two, three . . . now, Aiden, I really mean it" routine?

One way to find out how obedient your children are right now is to enter a room they are in and, looking at them, ask them to come to you. Do they look up and begin moving in your direction immediately without whining, complaining, or hesitation? If so, you are in good shape. If not, there may be some room for improvement.

An excellent, nonthreatening way to introduce this concept to a young family is to have a family home evening where the principle of obedience is introduced and explained in a nonconfrontational way. This can be done with a simple game. The children are invited to sit in a circle near the parent and then are asked one by one to come to the parent. When they obey, they are given a small treat. The game is repeated, but this time the children are asked to sit farther away. Again, using the same kind and gentle voice, each child is called in turn to come to the parent. Again the treat is offered. Finally, the children are asked to slip just out of sight of the parent and wait their turn to be called and come. Children are then invited to come when they are called for the rest of the evening, then the next day, and so on during the rest of the week, with small treats offered every time they are compliant and obedient. Eventually the treats could be replaced with affirming hugs and kisses, compliments, and validating statements.

Older children can also be taught the principles of obedience in a family council. Remember there are three keys to teaching obedience. First, look at your children when you speak to them. (All too often you are instructing your children to do something when you are occupied with other activities.) Second, wait and watch, still looking at them, until they obey you. (When you are first training your children, wait until you are obeyed every time. This is how they come to understand that you are really serious the first time, every time. Eventually, they will know that you mean business when you speak and they will not need to be watched so carefully.)

When your children understand that you mean what you say and they begin to obey regularly, it is important to continue to ask them to come back and report to you.

"John, I don't think I need to be with you when you put away your laundry anymore. We have worked together for a week, you seem to get the idea, you usually do it without fussing, and so I would like to just have you tell me when you are finished, and then you may leave to play with your friends. Pretty soon we won't even have to do that because when you ask me if you can go out to play, I will know that means you have already put away your laundry. That's called trust."

Finally, give them some reason to obey you. Initially, of course, that may need to be some small treat given at family council when each member practices obedience, as explained previously. Later on it can be generous praise and validation that their contributions are significant. This will often be sufficient impetus to carry older children to more constant obedience.

Children are very sensitive to your moods and know intuitively that they are in control when they can bring you to an angry state, so it is imperative to control your temper at all times. Speak with a calm voice, repeating if necessary the desired result you are seeking, and continue to wait and watch until you are obeyed.

Remember, if you want to stay in control of the situation, don't raise the volume or change the pitch of your voice. Don't resort to common intimidation practices, such as using their full names. While it is important to be firm, and sometimes necessary to describe how you are beginning to feel, self-restraint and self-control bring more long-term benefits to your family than the short-term benefits of blowing off steam.

In the end, children usually forget *why* you were mad, but readily remember that you *were* an angry parent. In turn, they will often repeat your patterns when they raise their own little ones. Wouldn't you like to improve your interactions with your children now so that family life can be more peaceful and calm?

As you work with your children to increase their desire and capacity to obey, remember there is great value in complimenting your children. Generally, it is most useful to compliment the child directly.

"Matt, thanks for coming in from your game and setting the table. I really appreciate knowing that you will keep your word."

Then compliment their behavior in a conversation with your spouse in the child's presence.

"Honey, this afternoon I was so happy with Matt when I called him in from playing with his friends. He told me he needed just a few more minutes to finish up his basketball game. I said okay, and he kept his word, came in, and set the table for dinner."

And finally, compliment them indirectly but within their hearing to another significant adult in their life such as a teacher or grandparent.

"Mom, I'm so glad you called . . . Matt and his friends had a good game of basketball yesterday, but I was especially pleased when he came in and set the table after he finished. Wow, it is great to have a son that I can depend on."

Can you see? Children will be just about as obedient as you expect them to be. If you insist that they come when they are first called and when you are still speaking in a normal voice (meaning you wait to be obeyed and follow up if you are not), and commend them if they come without resentment or frustration, you are well on your way to teaching them this valuable first lesson in becoming responsible adults.

When children have learned to obey their parents, they will begin functioning better at school, honoring older relatives, and getting along in public. It might not be easy to make this change in your family's interactions, but it is well worth it.

Honesty

This skill, like so many others, is first learned as children observe their own parents' behaviors. If you are honest in your work ethic, your children will be too. On the other hand, if they observe you being dishonest, it is likely that they will also try to slip by with less than true integrity. Children will have a hard time being honest when they hear a parent being dishonest. What example are you setting if your children hear you say, "Well, honey, the boss left at 3 P.M. today and so I snuck out early too and ran some errands on the way home."

As you train your children to work, and you provide them with the opportunity to learn other essential skills, they need to depend on your frank appraisal of how they are doing at any given moment, and you need to know that when they say they have done a job, they finished it completely and to the standard that you set. The idea is to create a mutual feeling of honesty between parent and child. You can trust each other because, as a parent, you won't say a job is done all right one time and then criticize the same level of work the next. In turn, children won't lie to get out of work so they can go play with friends sooner.

It is best to speak to your children about this concept openly. Be frank about what you expect when you begin to train them to do a job. Be open with mistakes they may make (kindly, of course). Talk about how much you depend on them to be honest once you trust them to complete a job appropriately before they say, "It's done."

Of course, from time to time your children will try to get by with a shoddy, incomplete attempt. It is then that you must be your strongest. You can't let small failings pass lightly. They must be addressed and the child encouraged to return to honest behavior. In turn, you must be candid in your conversation and open in your views.

"Michael, it is your chore to put away the clean dishes in the dishwasher in the morning before you leave to play with friends. I'm here at your friend's house because the dishwasher is still full of dishes. Let's hurry home so you can make things right, okay?"

After children understand how to be obedient and continue to practice being honest, they can learn other values that will help them in all aspects of their lives.

As you teach honesty to your children, you will become aware of some of your own less-than-honest behavior. When that happens, apologize to your children and let them know that you are "trying again." This helps them know that personal progress is a journey and that when they fail, they can try again too.

The Bedroom, a Mini-Home

Because children spend a lot of time in their bedrooms (about one-third of their young life is spent sleeping), and because it means a great deal to them to have some personal space, a bedroom is a good place to help them understand both the rudiments of all household work and the need for occasional deep-cleaning chores.

Initially, you use their bedrooms to teach children how to bring a room back to order. A sample "My Bedroom Chart" on page 55 details what needs to be done in a bedroom to restore it to order daily. (This chart is also available as a free download at www.houseoforder.com.) Because children often seem lost about how to do jobs (even after they have been thoroughly trained), it is useful to use My Bedroom Chart to remind them of the particular tasks that need to be done to keep their bedrooms orderly.

My Bedroom Chart can be marked off day after day and sometimes week after week as a way to keep children on task. For example, when this chart is all marked off and you have inspected the work, then the child is free to eat breakfast and go off to school, or to a friend's house if you choose to have chores done in the afternoon. As an alternative method, this information can be printed, laminated, and then kept as a reference card for everyday use.

When children have mastered the routine and skills to straighten their bedrooms every day and you feel they are doing it successfully, add other skills. You can teach them how to do similar chores in their bedrooms as you are doing around the house. This will offer them the opportunity to experience some of the more difficult skills of home maintenance by practicing these jobs in their bedrooms.

For example, if you are washing your windows inside and out, they could participate, even at a young age, with helping you do the windows in their bedrooms. If you are dusting door frames, they could dust their door frames, both inside and out. If you are spot cleaning the carpets, they could learn to spot clean their bedroom carpet.

If you are taking down all the blinds in your home for cleaning in the bathtub, rinsing them outside in the backyard, and then rehanging them when they are dried, let your children participate in some way when it is time to do their blinds. If you are changing the sheets, let them help you strip the sheets from their beds. If you are dusting the baseboards around the house, have them dust the baseboards in their bedrooms.

In other words, any time you do a major, more complex job around the house, use this opportunity to teach them how to do this job in their bedrooms. Not only will they gain confidence as they do a smaller part of the bigger jobs, but they will have more ownership of their bedrooms' maintenance.

My bedroom is NEAT today when . . .

- ☐ I have made my bed.

- ☐ I have folded my extra blankets and put them neatly at the end of my bed.

- ☐ I have put my pillows at the head of my bed.

- ☐ I have picked up everything from the bedroom floor.

- ☐ I have straightened my desk.

- ☐ I have cleaned off the top of the chest of drawers.

- ☐ I have put my dirty clothes in the laundry basket.

- ☐ I have hung up all my clean clothes in the closet.

- ☐ I have put my shoes neatly away in my closet.

- ☐ I have put all my trash in the wastebasket.

- ☐ I have checked one more time to make sure there is nothing out of place in my bedroom.

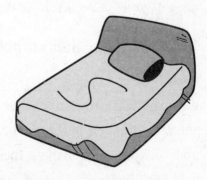

CHAPTER SEVEN

For Children Ages 2-6, a Time to Teach and Love

Children don't do what you expect—they do what you inspect.

Children need to learn how to work. It is essential to their very survival as adults and to their success as parents. Generally, you first teach them how to be obedient, encourage their honesty, show them how to straighten their rooms on a regular basis, and let them routinely participate in more complex chores by doing similar chores in their bedrooms. Next, it is useful to think of further job training by dividing a child's life into three seasons: preschool, elementary school, and secondary school. For most children, those divisions fall into the age categories of 2–6, 6–12, and 12–18.

Setting Up for Self-sufficiency

Whenever possible, as you prepare to train your children how to work, create an environment that promotes self-sufficiency. I often call this the "principle of the stool." For example, if you, as a parent, are asked by your children to get them a drink of water and you do so, you are like a fisherman who catches a fish and then feeds it to his children.

If you purchase or make a stool, teach your children how to climb up on it, have a simple system for them to find, reach out, and pick up their cup from a wall hook system, you are beginning to teach them to become self-sufficient. If you continue to show them how to pour the water they don't want to drink into the sink, help them put their cups back on their own hooks, show them how to step down from the stool safely and then put the stool away in its "home," you are training them how to finish their tasks within their own realm of self-sufficiency.

It is for this reason that you do all you can to make children's lives and their tasks such that they can be independent. You put a closet rod lower so children can learn to hang up their own clothes. You purchase or make a simple sleeping bag to use on top of the fitted sheet on their bed so bed making is easy. You show them how to use a napkin so their face and immediate table area remain clean when they eat. In so many ways, you promote self-sufficiency by bringing your world down to your children's level so they can function to the highest degree without your help or interference.

One wise parent slowly moved around his home on his knees to see the home more clearly from his children's level. It was then that he moved the children's books to bookshelves where they were at the eye level of his preschool-age sons; he bought stools for all the bathrooms; he rearranged things so their personal bedroom drawers were below their elbow level for easier organizing. He looked at their world from their viewpoint and realized that it would be easier for him, as a parent, to train his children how to work when they could more easily access the things they used.

Personal Hygiene Habits

New habits come slowly, but they can last a lifetime. Teach and train your children from the very beginning so that good habits are well-established routines in their lives. Not only are the habits themselves important, but so are the patterns of discipline, order, and attention to detail that result from learning how to do a job right. Even if you are working with an older child or teenager, make sure that these foundational habits are in place before you continue on to more complex training. By starting out right, the habits can build upon themselves and provide impetus for all future work situations.

The best place to start training children is with personal hygiene habits. Even an infant can learn by simply listening to voices and watching actions. For some time after children are born, you will be attending to all of their personal hygiene needs. Even as you do so, you can verbalize what is happening, why you are doing it, and what will be happening next. Of course, sweet parental oohs and aaahs will make the experience all the more pleasurable for the child.

> "Katie, isn't it nice to climb into a warm bath? First we wash your face, then your hair. Then we wipe around your eyes, nose, mouth, and ears. Your shoulders, arms, and hands come next. Your tummy and back need a nice rub, too. Finally, we will wash down each leg, give each foot a scrub, and then we are all done taking a bath."

Parents who talk as they interact with and take care of their children will find that they are teaching even as they care for a babe in arms. The child is being exposed to new vocabulary words, the patterns for doing a particular part of daily routines, and the love that comes through the voice and touch. Order and method will be imprinted in the child's mind.

All too soon, your children will be in the bathtub playing all on their own, but the pattern of learning will continue.

"Jeremy, you've sure had fun playing in the bathtub. Now it's time to put your tub toys in the rack. There's the fisherman. Let's put him in his 'ship.' Can you put the whale in the rack? I found the starfish. Where is that diver? He'll need to sleep in the ship, too, until tomorrow's bath.

"Now, let's get your body as clean as the fisherman's. We'll start with your face, then do your ears, around your neck, down the left arm, then down the right arm, around your stomach and back, and then down your right leg, and finally down your left leg. Let's get some soap in between your toes. A good rinse will get the soap off and leave your skin shiny clean."

Can you see how you are teaching left-right coordination, the patterns for bathing properly, and loving the child all at the same time? Parents can always be teaching and training, verbalizing the patterns, the beginning and end of a project, and the need for personal hygiene with daily dedication and care.

"Abby, doesn't this fluffy towel feel good? We'll wrap it snugly around you for a bit and then start to get all the water off. First we'll dry your face, then we'll wipe off your arms, down your body, and then down your right leg and then your left leg. Now we'll fluff your hair dry and soon you'll be ready to get into your underwear and pajamas."

As children express a desire for independence, you can begin talking about what they can do on their own when they feel they are old enough.

"Jared, every night we work together to pick up the bath toys and put them in the drying rack. Soon you will be old enough to put the toys away all on your own. I'm looking forward to that time. It will mean that you are growing up."

After several days of teaching about independence, you might put Jared into the tub with a gentle suggestion.

> "Is today the day when you will put your toys away all by your-self? That will be a big step toward becoming independent. I'm sure you are looking forward to that day, and I am too."

(As a side note, don't worry about using big words around little children. They pick up the meaning and innuendos of longer words almost as quickly as shorter ones and quickly end up with a larger vocabulary. Just talk to them as you would any adult. If they ask, explain. If they don't, just keep talking like you normally do. Children are usually smarter than most adults assume.)

Helping Out Habits

As soon as children can make a mess, it is time to begin training them to clean up their mess. This is a large part of job training. In other words, what children mess up, they should help clean up. It might initially be picking up pieces of the cold cereal that have been flung from a high chair, but talk it through and request help.

> "Jonah, when we throw cereal, we must also pick it up. I see a pink circle there. It belongs in this bowl. Thanks. Now, I see a blue circle here. Thanks, sweetie, for picking up the 'lost' cereal."

In the same way, you begin to have children participate in daily chores. Initially their responsibilities will be easy to do, but it is important that they are clearly identified and completed on a daily basis. This consistent contribution to the running of the household helps children understand their usefulness to the family. They begin to comprehend that they can make a difference, and thus their self-esteem grows.

For instance, young children might be in charge of taking their silverware and dropping it in the sink after meals. Later they will be in charge of putting their dishes in the dishwasher. As they grow and develop, they might also be in charge of putting away the salt and pepper, clearing the rest of the table, and then helping to clean up the kitchen after meals.

As children mature, their jobs become more complex, longer, and more detailed. The important principles, however, are always the same. Children are taught what to do, are shown how to do it, are watched while they do it, and are encouraged, always encouraged, to move toward total self-initiative to complete their jobs.

Discarding Habits

Children need to learn how to discard unneeded items. This is an essential habit in and of itself, but it is also important to know how to get the discarded item successfully into the appropriate container. Start with training your very young children how to put larger objects in a wastebasket.

 "Jordan, here is how we put an empty catsup container in the kitchen wastebasket. First we close the lid of the bottle. Then we place it down into the wastebasket so that it won't fall outside. We don't just drop it in. Placing it in the wastebasket keeps other things in the wastebasket from coming out.

"Now, let's practice putting this empty catsup bottle in the wastebasket? Yes, that's right. Close the lid. Put it down inside quite close to the other items, and then let it go. What a nice job, Jordan. Thanks for helping me."

Sometimes it will feel like you are over-explaining simple parts of a task, but all wise parents know that it is easier to over-explain initially than to clean up a mess later or to have a chronic problem with children who didn't learn right the first time and now refuse to do it right any time.

Self-initiative Habits

Children should not only know personal hygiene skills and how to clean up after themselves, but also how to complete these simple tasks using their own initiative. When they are grown, you shouldn't have to follow them around saying, "Did you remember to flush the toilet?" "Did you hand in your research paper today?" "Did you turn off the stove after fixing dinner?" Since you want your children to grow up to be competent and independent, it is essential to move them toward complete independence with every possible interaction.

> "Josh, you have committed to empty the kitchen wastebasket every day. What is the best way for you to remember this responsibility without being reminded by me?"

Surprisingly, children have creative responses. Support them as they learn to do their jobs right, do them completely, and, most important, do them without being reminded, prodded, or nagged.

Parents who train their children, follow up on their children's performance, want their children to act independently, and praise them generously will find that their children will not only contribute significantly to their family's housework, but will also be able to tackle adult activities with greater competence. They will have the capacity to get a full-time job and keep it, marry, and raise a family because they have been doing a smaller part of these very tasks their whole lives.

Beginning Work Skills

When children are very young—in fact, as soon as they begin to comprehend language at all—it is useful to describe the rudiments of all that you do during the day and to establish in your children's minds the rules and routines that you follow. Then when it is time to actually train your children, they will already know that their parents do chores, that they do it in a certain way, and that they work with a pattern. Young children are especially observant and learn more quickly if the parent actually does the job for them first to show them how it is done. Explaining each step of the process as you go along is also helpful. Then the job is explained again as it is completed by the children.

In the beginning, they will need to learn simple terms and their corresponding actions. For example:

"Tom, we shut the door after we have opened it. See, open the door, shut the door, open the door, shut the door."

When Tom is a toddler this is a game of open, shut, open, shut. But as you play with him, you are training him that doors can open and shut and that shutting happens at the end.

There are many additional, simple work terms that need to be explained and demonstrated to the child. These include skills such as "turn on/turn off," "pick up/put down," "put away/throw away," "unfold/fold," and "pull out/push in." As these terms are explained as part of your everyday conversation, you might include the standards that work best in your home.

"Jana, when we enter a room we turn on the light. Here, let me pick you up, and you can turn on the light to your bedroom. When we leave the room we turn off the light. Of course you can turn the light off when we leave!"

"We pick up our dirty clothes after we have undressed and we put them in the dirty clothes hamper. Samantha, I think you are big enough to pick up your socks and I'll pick up your top and pants. Now, where is that dirty clothes hamper? Oh, you found it. Can you hold the top open while I put these dirty clothes in it? Then you can put your socks in there, too."

"Brian, sometimes we put things away and sometimes we throw them away. Let's put away this magazine in the magazine rack and let's throw yesterday's newspaper in the recycle bin in the garage. I'll hold the magazine; you can hold the newspapers."

"Sarah, you are right, it is good to pull out your chair before you climb onto it for dinner. It is also good to push the chairs back softly against the table when we are finished eating. It makes the dining area look neat and nice until the next meal. Everyone else has an after-dinner job. I think you are old enough to help, too. Pushing in the chairs would certainly be a big help to the whole family. Would you be willing to do it tonight?"

"Jack, we unfold the towels when we are ready to hang them on the towel rack in the kitchen. If we fold them up just right when they come out of the dryer clean and dry, they will be easier to hang. May I show you how to fold towels and then show you where we put them in the kitchen drawer? . . . Now you can fold the kitchen towels while I fold the bathroom ones."

Over and over and over again, you are helping children prepare for formal chore responsibilities as you explain the simple tasks that keep your home organized and clean and then request their help.

Tell Them How, Show Them How, and Watch Them Do

When training very young children, each step of the process should be explained as you model the procedures for completing the job. During this part of the training, children are watching and internalizing. They then perform the job themselves, usually five times or more, with parental supervision, compliments, and correction. The children continue to internalize and duplicate the new skills you have demonstrated. Next they are encouraged to do the job five more times without supervision, but with parental inspection, more compliments, and consistent correction. At this point, they independently do the job, return and report their success, and then receive parental compliments and occasional rewards to keep them motivated.

Remember, children desire many things, but one of the most important is to please you. They desire to contribute in the home because it makes them feel loved, needed, and wanted. It is their way of saying thank you. They may not completely understand this concept initially or even consciously, but everyone wants to be valued for their capacity to donate their time and energy even—and especially—when they are very young.

Let's look at Max, who is being taught how to hang his coat on a hanger.

"Max, it is time for you to hang up your own coat. You have seen Dad and me hang up our coats, and for many months I have hung up your coat when you hand it to me when we get home from the playground. But look at you, you are getting very tall now, and I think you can reach a hanger on the lower closet rod.

"See, you can . . . Now let me show you how to hang up your coat. The neck of your coat goes against the neck of the hanger. The shoulders of your coat go over the elbows of the hanger, just so. Now we hold the coat neck and the hanger neck tightly together as we take our other hand and push open a place in the closet for your coat.

"I have seen you do many hard things, Max. Let's see how much of this you can do alone."

Now Max, being a normal child, might balk at learning a new skill. A little persuasion is always good. It might take the form of an edible treat. It might be the promise of a story to be read. It might be the opportunity to play with some treasured toys. It might even be telling him a creative story about the big bear coat that needs a friend so it can play and how glad it is to be put into the deep forest of other coats so it can have someone to play with.

In the case of hesitant children, you might say,

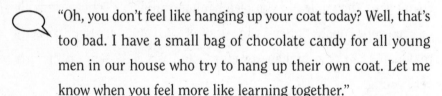

"Oh, you don't feel like hanging up your coat today? Well, that's too bad. I have a small bag of chocolate candy for all young men in our house who try to hang up their own coat. Let me know when you feel more like learning together."

Now, Max might still not be persuaded by candy, reading, or toys. In that case, you must hold off these promised treasures until he has successfully practiced the behavior you desired. Just occasionally remind him that chocolate candy are waiting for the bear coat to be put with the other bears in the closet forest so they can play together.

Children usually need to complete a specified job five or more times with parental supervision before they are competent to do it themselves. Then the children are given the opportunity to complete the job five or more times with only parental inspection and additional compliments.

When the parent feels confident the children know how to hang up their coats, know when it is to be hung up, and complete this job successfully, the children are left to do the job with only occasional supervision, a treat here and there to help with motivation, and generous and frequent praise.

It is very important to understand that training children in the right way to do a job and then rewarding them sufficiently with compliments and congratulations will do more to ensure the job will be completed successfully in the future than just about any other method.

It takes a lot of time and energy to do a job five times with children, to get them to do it alone five times with your inspection, approval, and praise, and then to let them complete the job on an ongoing basis, returning and reporting, and then receiving your occasional supervision and consistent praise. However, there is nothing like "you're making a significant contribution" compliments to make children feel wanted and needed.

At the beginning, it is enough to have one designated job for each year of the child's age. The jobs for young children would best be daily jobs, ones they will do every day. They might include personal grooming jobs such as dressing themselves, combing their hair, brushing their teeth, washing their face, and putting their shoes and clothes away when they get into their pajamas. Two-year-old Lily has two jobs of her own, maybe washing her face in the morning and folding her towel after her bath. As children gain competency and interest, more jobs can be added according to their abilities, even beyond the initial number of jobs you may have given them. This does not mean children do not have other responsibilities, but these specific ones are called "their" jobs. Three-year-old David, for instance, will have at least three identifiable jobs that he can talk about. Even if he can't articulate those jobs clearly he knows the following: "I'm in charge of combing my hair in the morning. I put my dirty clothes in the laundry basket when I bathe at night. I put my shoes in my bedroom shoe container when I get in my pajamas. These are my jobs."

When children turn four, or when it is obvious they can contribute more to the success of the household, they can be given more formal jobs. For instance, Ashley is four and will have at least four jobs to call her own. She might make her bed in the morning, comb her hair, get dressed all by herself (except for tying her shoes), and push the chairs in after breakfast. Each and every skill that is learned becomes part of her contribution to the family and is part of her daily routine. This will increase her capacity to be a contributing member of the family.

It is important during these early years to have the same assigned jobs every day of the week. You are trying to build consistent behaviors, regular routines, and repetitive obedience.

Remember, introduce personal grooming jobs first. Over and over again you walk and talk through how to do these jobs right. You accept any and all help doing these grooming tasks until the children can become independent in doing these chores themselves.

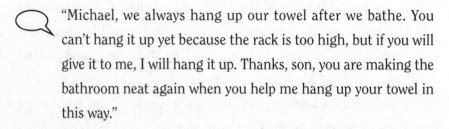

"Michael, we always hang up our towel after we bathe. You can't hang it up yet because the rack is too high, but if you will give it to me, I will hang it up. Thanks, son, you are making the bathroom neat again when you help me hang up your towel in this way."

As you compliment children for the contributions they can make, you also speak about the next step in the behavior you desire.

"Michael, I'm so glad you are willing to pick up your towel so I can hang it up. Pretty soon, when you are a little taller, you will be able to hang your towel up all by yourself. As a matter of fact, I think it will be only a couple of months until you will be able to reach the rack all by yourself. Try reaching right now. See . . . you are almost tall enough. That will be a fun day when you hang up your own towel just like I do."

After personal grooming jobs are introduced, work to train children on how to straighten their personal environments. Since, in many respects, children's bedrooms (or part of a bedroom) represent their "mini" home, their ability and willingness to keep their own small world orderly will be a good beginning to keeping in order larger portions of the home, their personal lives, and eventually larger, more important responsibilities.

For this reason, when more formal job training begins, it is important to completely train children how to straighten up their bedrooms each and every morning when they arise. You might include such jobs as making their beds, emptying the wastebasket, lining up their books, pushing in their desk chairs, shutting their bedroom closet doors, and opening their window coverings.

Remember, if children can get toys out and make a mess, they are agile enough to clean up after themselves. Of course, initially, this will take a lot of parental involvement because children work better when they have adult help. After several times of working with them and then several more times watching them work, you can eventually tell them to complete the job and report their progress to you.

Next, train young children to do rudimentary jobs in other parts of the house that teach them to move from chaos to order. These jobs might include participating in any and all housework that you do. When you are folding the laundry, they can separate out the towels, fold washcloths, hang up shirts, or match socks. When you are cleaning up after a meal, they could put the pepper and salt shakers away, push in the chairs around the table, or sweep up the crumbs under the high chair. You do not want them to do jobs that will always take a long time, but instead make sure they do easier jobs on a consistent basis so they can identify that they do contribute in certain, specific ways.

Finally, preschool-age children can be taught how to do preliminary scholarly activities such as writing their names, memorizing their address and phone number (an essential job for children before they leave the home to attend school or classes of any kind), writing the numbers 0–10 (and beyond), learning their colors, and reading on a most basic level. Every skill children learn can be identified as a daily "job" they do over and over again to increase their capabilities in life.

 "Oh, Josh, you have learned to write your first name. You have been writing it every day for a week now. Soon you will be able to write your last name, too. Then I'll teach you how to write our address and phone number. Wow, what an accomplishment to be able to write out these important facts yourself!"

Depending on the configuration of your family, you might involve your older preschool children in training younger siblings in these rudimentary jobs. For example, a five-year-old child might be encouraged to teach the three-year-old the colors. In this way, older children retain this information to an even greater degree as they, in turn, share their knowledge.

 "Brody, I'm so glad you know your colors. Carly doesn't, though. While we are waiting for the doctor to see us, can I point to something and you tell her the color? See, here is a silk plant. What color are the leaves? Carly, can you say 'green' like Brody just did? See, Brody, you are a teacher now. You know your colors and can share them with everyone else who doesn't know."

As you train your children, remember to make this process fun, easy, and meaningful. Children respond rapidly to parents who enjoy their own work, and most love a bit of creativity added to a routine.

> "Jack and Sam, today when we clean the kitchen let's pretend it is a zoo. Jack, you are in charge of wiping down the chairs. Since they are black and white, let's call the chairs zebras today. Sam, since you are in charge of sweeping the floor, let's pretend you are cleaning out the elephant's cage. I'm washing the dishes and I want to pretend that I'm the peanut and popcorn vendor cleaning up her supplies. When we have our zoo spic-and-span, we will pop some popcorn and take a well-deserved zookeepers' break."

Because small and simple beginnings result in large, far-reaching behaviors, taking the time to train children using the right method with a regular routine gives them feelings of reward and self-fulfillment that are worth all the time and trouble it takes. Most children respond positively to such attention and the feelings of well-being that come as they do their part to make a home function smoothly.

And occasionally, just to make sure surprises are a part of their lives, give your children an afternoon off to watch a favorite movie with a friend or permission to share an evening with extended family members. Letting them leave work to play, just once in a while, is also an important part of life's pleasures.

CHAPTER EIGHT

For Children Ages 6–12, a Time to Train and Support

If you want to train your children how to work correctly, you must break down each new task into small parts and demonstrate each part step by step.

I'm sure you, as a parent, are anxious for your children, no matter their current ages, to grow up to be strong, independent, fully functioning adults. You want them to have self-initiative, to be hardworking, to be honest, and to be diligent. You want them to be something special.

When children move to the years between six and twelve, there is an increased number of outside influences on their behavior: more friends and numerous extracurricular activities. Their attitudes and responses to parental control and training change and sometimes become less positive. You hope your children have already performed enough jobs on a regular basis around the house that they will respond positively to new and bigger responsibilities as they mature. It is important that you continue to train your children how to work and increase their skill base and encourage their continued contribution to the ordering, cleaning, and maintenance of your home and yard. Children need this consistent responsibility to feel familial security and to have structure in their personal lives. Your children come to feel they are important because they are essential to the everyday functioning of your family.

For the most part, children of these elementary-school ages are accountable for their personal grooming; it has become a part of their routine and no longer needs to be monitored except occasionally. Therefore, different and more difficult "making things neat" jobs can be introduced as your children mature. The goal is to help children become accountable for doing their jobs, initiate their completion without being reminded, and take pride in their work.

The complete list of skills that you feel your children will need as they mature into adults is detailed in chapter 5. Having this Master Plan on lined index cards makes it possible to move the job cards around on a table as you decide which children will do which jobs during the upcoming school year, an upcoming summer, or maybe even an upcoming stressful time when they will need to carry more than the normal share of housework.

Because training school-age children to work is best done with a minimum of distractions and pressures, it may prove useful to use each summer vacation to train your children in more of these various skills. Naturally, there will be weeks when you are on vacation, maybe a group of days when they are away at camp, and even a weekend when you all take a break from major housework because Grandma is in town. But between those times, it is useful for children to learn and grow in household skills. And it is up to you to train them, to supervise the completion of their assigned jobs, and even to correct them as necessary. Most important, it is your opportunity to compliment their successes, their increased speed, and their improved quality of work.

It is helpful if each child in your family is involved in ordering, cleaning, and even scrubbing parts of your home and yard during these summer training months. (If your children are on a year-round school schedule, these same skills can be taught during off-school times.) Children might be involved in dusting part of the house, vacuuming a room, cleaning part of the bathroom(s), and scrubbing part of the kitchen. They should also be involved in doing the laundry, fixing meals, cleaning up afterward, and helping with yard work.

I can feel your stress level rising as you read this. It is a lot of work to organize your children to do household chores, sometimes even more work than just doing them yourself. But it is part of your stewardship as a parent to teach them to be adults, to work toward being parents, and to mature into functioning human beings that make significant contributions to society, home, and their chosen careers. This potential is nurtured as you train them to do simple jobs at home.

New jobs are best introduced during school vacation months when the atmosphere is relaxed and time permits thorough training and follow-through on your part. Although children catch on very quickly during the ages of six to twelve, as you train your children to work, it is best to break down each new job into small tasks and demonstrate them step-by-step. It is also helpful to write out the details of different jobs on Standards charts (see pages 40–47).

For instance, if you are training your eleven-year-old daughter how to clean a bathroom, she needs to understand exactly how you want her to shine the mirrors, wipe down the counter and top of the toilet, clean the sink, scrub the tub, sweep and wipe up the floor, and clean the toilet. These are the smaller steps to completing the bigger bathroom-cleaning job. Use the Standards charts to indicate what each job entails and then demonstrate how to clean the bathroom.

After your school-age children have watched you clean the

bathroom, have done it alone with your supervision three or more times, and have finished cleaning the bathroom three times alone with parental inspection, post-training, and sincere compliments, they can become independent. Continue to monitor their work by having them report back to you, and always give compliments and an occasional treat to make the job more pleasant to tackle and complete.

Again, it is not so important that children be working for long hours during their summer vacation. On the contrary, let them have a spread of responsibilities that will allow them exposure to all kinds of housework, cooking several meals a week, helping with the laundry, and aiding with the yard work. Have smaller time commitments for younger children and reasonable periods of work for older children. Teenagers can make significant contributions at home until they begin to work outside the home during summer months. Remember, having regular household jobs brings with it reliable routines, superior habits, and the potential for improved behavior.

It really doesn't take that much time to keep the house in order, get the laundry done, keep the meals prepared, and finish the yard work if everyone has their individual responsibilities and is competently completing them. It is individual responsibility that leads to group success. As a parent you are the trainer, the director, the corrector, and the cheerleader, all wrapped into one. You are essential to the training of your children, especially when it comes to schooling them in how to work.

Of course, that means you will need a system for motivation, a system for inspection, and a system for reward, but creative families come up with ways to help themselves through these challenges. You will find that your children will have interesting suggestions to maintain motivation, accept your inspection comments, and receive rewards. Usually, they are their own best taskmasters.

"Connor, you have accepted the jobs of dusting the front room, vacuuming the foyer and front stairs, and wiping the half-bath counters each morning. I can remind you about these jobs all summer, or we can figure out a way for you to remind yourself and get a reward for being independent so I don't need to oversee your work. I have noticed that you are becoming quite mature, that you do your jobs completely to the end, and that you can be counted on. How can I help you remember to do your jobs each morning before you go out to play?"

Each and every time children begin a job with their own initiative, complete a job well, and receive sufficient praise for their work, they become more and more confident of finding their place in the world. One of the best gifts you can give your children is teaching them the value, wonder, and feeling of a job well done.

Choose the skills you would like them to learn, teach them diligently during the summer months, let them retain their favorite jobs during the school year, and then repeat the process again with more difficult and more complex jobs the next summer. Soon your children will become quite adultlike. They may complain occasionally (and maybe even frequently, if it is a bad week), but they will also be looked up to by others as they become more and more independent, dependable, and competent because of their training at home.

During a long year in my own life, my husband and four sons had to completely take over our household affairs while I was in the hospital with our baby, who was struggling with an acute form of leukemia. Jim sat down with the boys, discussed the situation, and asked for their contributions. Using the Master Plan, they made a list of essential daily and weekly jobs that needed to be done. One of our younger son's contributions was the daily sweeping and then weekly mopping of the small, tile entryway of our home. This tile area was just four feet by four feet in size. However, even to this day, he remembers how he helped out at home "while Evan was in the hospital." Our older sons took on more complex jobs, from making their beds and straightening their rooms before they left for school, to helping clean these and other rooms in the house on Saturday. My husband worked with them, complimented and corrected them, and together they maintained the house while I nursed our baby, took care of complicated hospital procedures, and more or less lived with our sick infant in the hospital.

After Evan's death, I returned to our home and we made major adjustments in the housekeeping responsibilities of our sons. They still worked hard, but now things were a bit different, and more of the housework load shifted to my shoulders again. They continued to straighten their rooms each day and clean a smaller portion of the house each week, but I returned to more of the organizing, cooking, and cleaning in the home.

It will be the same in your home. Always allow your children to contribute, but shift the burden as circumstances require. A broken leg might confine a child for a while, but he can continue to contribute to a successful home, just in a different way. Maybe he will be in charge of folding laundry for two people and another sibling will take over his bathroom cleaning chores while being relieved of folding laundry. Maybe he will be the "reader" to the younger children and they will be his "legs."

Can you see how training your children to work—even as you shift the responsibilities as changes come to your lives—will help them, again and again, to mature into competent, capable, adaptive youth and eventually sterling adults? All the work, diligence, and long hours of correction and complimenting will be worth your time and trouble.

School Time

When children return to school, they should retain at least one "official" job for each year of their age. Some jobs appropriate for this age group during the school months include emptying the dishwasher and putting the dishes away, cleaning the mirror and basin in the bathroom each morning, cleaning up toys before dinner, and helping with the dinner dishes.

The bedroom is also a good place to help children continue to be responsible for their own miniature "homes." Morning jobs such as making their beds, opening the bedroom curtains, cleaning up toys and clothes, and closing drawers and closet doors make for a better beginning of the day for the whole household and also establish habits that can be beneficial for a lifetime.

Occasional Jobs

Children between six and twelve are mature enough to remember to do a job that happens only occasionally during the week. Some weekly jobs to consider are putting garbage cans out on the curb on Thursday evening, washing the car on Saturdays, putting the laundry away on Monday, Wednesday, and Friday, and changing their sheets on Fridays. Other jobs that are done on an "as needed" basis might also be added, such as raking leaves in the fall, weeding the shrubs in the spring, or sweeping the walks after a windy rainstorm.

Finally, it is during these years that children can be trained in the rudiments of repairing. They should learn how and when to use glue, clamps, wire, and duct tape. They need to understand how to take a tool apart carefully so it can be put back together successfully after it has been repaired. They will need to become more competent in more complex activities.

In summary, between the ages of six and twelve, your children should receive continued training, learn to follow instructions, act independently, and successfully complete their assignments. These skills will be very beneficial when they enter the real working world during the formative teenage years.

CHAPTER NINE

For Youth Ages 12-18, a Time to Become Independent

As parents, your job is to work yourselves out of a job by helping your children become productive, happy, and responsible adults.

The last six years of training are vital to your maturing children. This is especially true because their interest in adultlike behavior is paramount and their need to assume more and more responsibility is essential. If they have been trained well during their formative years, teenagers will take care of their personal grooming and bedroom-straightening jobs of their own accord. Sometimes they do not take care of their room as you would wish, but it is important to agree upon a bedroom cleaning schedule and go from there. In other words, you will give gentle suggestions, monitoring, and praise, but this part of their lives is not necessarily considered part of their official family jobs.

Regular Jobs

Young people should continue to have regular daily and weekly family jobs although they may be heavily involved in school, work outside the home, and other extracurricular activities. This is because, in real life, when they are on their own, they will also have household responsibilities, whether they are going to school or holding down a job. They should also participate occasionally in the difficult and complex jobs around the house so they will become skilled at them and can keep a balance in their own lives both now and in the future. One of the harder challenges youth have when they leave the home is keeping track of what needs to be done, having the motivation to do it when they don't feel like it, and getting it done in a timely manner.

Independence Jobs

"Independence" jobs are those that require more muscle and finesse, usually are not done on a daily basis, and yet are essential to running a home. Teenagers are very capable of doing this type of grown-up work in addition to regular, routine housework. Cleaning the kitchen on a weekly basis, doing their own laundry, or fixing a complete meal are skills well within the capacity of youth this age. Continue to encourage the self-initiative you have tried to instill in your children during the first twelve years of their lives. If they do their jobs consistently on their own now, you have indeed been successful in helping them mature into productive adults.

Summer Jobs

Again, summertime is the best time to introduce new, more complex jobs to teenagers. As your children move through their teen years, they should take more responsibility for running the house, preparing meals, cleaning up after themselves and younger siblings, and taking the initiative to do whatever work needs to be done around the house or yard even if they have not received a formal assignment.

Teens can be a little sensitive about receiving instruction from their parents, so after the initial introduction to a job, they will usually refer to the Standards chart to make sure they did the job completely and properly when they do it alone for the first time. (See sample Standards charts on pages 40–47.) They'll probably call for you only when they are ready for the first inspection. If they complete the job correctly the first time, you might want to inspect their work on an occasional basis with compliments and surprise treats to keep the jobs fun and rewarding.

By the time teenagers are eighteen, they should have been introduced to all household chores (daily, weekly, occasional, and complex), have learned to complete them competently, and have been exposed to vehicle maintenance, mending their clothes, and cooking their own meals.

All the more difficult activities of home, yard, and vehicle maintenance should have been introduced and practiced. They should know how to check the oil and tire pressure of a vehicle and know how to renew a car's registration. They should be able to balance their banking account, make deposits, and handle a debit card and credit card successfully. They should regularly shop for groceries and prepare family meals without any help (although they will also enjoy company).

They should be ready to live successfully and completely on their own!

Self-management Skills

As your children mature and prepare to leave your home, there are specific important skills and habits that must be taught, reinforced, and practiced during their teenage years to more completely prepare them for the complexities of adult life. You will probably get a more positive response from your children if you work on these habits when they are twelve or thirteen rather than waiting until they are seventeen or eighteen. While these subjects have been touched on previously in this book, the following is a fairly comprehensive list of what you might consider as training opportunities for creating the best possible future for your maturing children.

Personal Habits

Young people maturing into adulthood should be independent in getting up and going to bed. You, of course, can set parameters for your family about when children need to be home and limits as to how late they may stay up, but within those parameters, your children should be self-sufficient in getting themselves up and in going to sleep at a reasonable time. Purchase personal alarm clocks for your children and train them how to use them. Discuss the usefulness of going to bed and getting up at the same times every day to settle their bodies into a cycle that makes for better overall health. Getting up and going to bed without supervision makes it easier for your teens to handle other difficult skills that require self-discipline and self-mastery. Naturally there will be some weekends and evenings when they will need to stay up later, but a consistent bedtime makes for healthier, happier, and more mentally alert young people.

The weekend is a good time to have your children practice getting up and going to bed independent of your input. They will then know how to use the alarm clock successfully when it does matter. Next, remove yourself from their waking cycle scene and, except for rare occasions, let them learn from their own experiences how to get up and go to school in a timely manner. This self-discipline is the beginning of personal skills that will be very useful to young adults.

Young people should routinely be making their beds and straightening their sleeping areas every morning. This is a small but important way for them to gain control of this part of their lives and maintain their personal orderliness. Share your own experiences about how being personally self-disciplined to make your bed, keeping your personal environment neat, and having these habits ingrained into your personal routines have helped you accomplish more in less time. If you struggle with these personal habits, working together as parent and teenager makes for fun dual-training sessions.

Exercise Habits

Adult experiences, including going away to school, working full time, and approaching a permanent relationship with another human being can be some of the more challenging experiences a young adult will face. Learning to deal with these stresses through consistent physical exercise is somewhat natural for the more active teenager, but should be encouraged for all teenagers so the habit is well instilled as they approach adulthood. A good, long exercise period each and every day will increase their bodies' capacity to do all other activities with more grace and focus. Stamina will increase, as will the skills to focus on difficult, complex mental activities. When the body is functioning at high capacity, so can the mind and the emotions.

Grooming Habits

Many of the grooming skills you taught your teens as children are well in place and have been practiced for many years. While they will have their own particular style (which will probably be very different from your own), encourage your teenagers to spruce up, be more neatly groomed, and dress above the standards of the crowd just a bit. It gives them an edge around teachers and other adults when they are dressed neatly.

Train your teenagers to dress appropriately for different occasions. A formal wedding reception, for example, requires a different set of clothes than a casual party at a park. From the beginning of their teenage years, help them see what works and what doesn't work on different occasions and that they can impress and honor their hosts when they dress appropriately for the situation. Discuss this in advance of the event so that you don't have a stand-off as you are leaving for the event (in which case you might not be successful at all if they refuse to change their clothes).

Because dress often becomes a way of self-expression during these teen years, you can help your teenagers express their individuality at the same time you help them keep within Church and family standards and values regarding modesty, body exposure, extreme dressing, and fabric type. Reiterate to your teens that neatly mended, modest clothing exudes a feeling of self-confidence that others can readily feel in their presence. The booklet *For the Strength of Youth* can be of great benefit here.

Hairstyles sometimes approach the extremes during these years and some of your children might move to the edge of what you can tolerate. Even as you decide what will work within your family standards, consider giving your children a bit of latitude in self-expression as they mature into adulthood. It is more important that you have neatness, cleanliness, and consistency than that you worry too much about their current, temporary hair color or style. If you have been conservative yourself and have taught them from their younger years to bathe daily, keep their fingernails clean and cut, their hair trimmed and clean, and their clothes maintained and mended, they will probably circle around again after their temporary need to experiment with their hair and clothing. In other words, train well, teach consistency, and be somewhat mellow as they discover themselves regarding personal grooming.

From time to time, especially when they have an important date or someone they want to impress, you will have a greater opportunity to encourage concepts you have previously taught.

In addition to their personal cleanliness, continue to encourage teenagers to straighten up the bathroom every time they use it. This will make for a more peaceful time at home now and with their college roommates or mission companions later, and it will be most appreciated by their spouses when they marry.

Trustworthy Habits

Continue to ensure discipline, especially if it is difficult for you to do so, when your teenagers purposefully break or ignore well-established family rules. To be trustworthy during these years is very important as they prepare to be on their own. They will sometimes ask for latitude in certain rules, especially when they feel they deserve it, and you might be willing to let them gain more and more independence as they prove worthy of it, but trustworthiness is an important, basic character trait they will want to have to be successful as adults.

Your teenagers are dealing daily with less eager and not-so-honest young people at school and work. Role playing and discussion can help them understand that being known as an honest, trustworthy young person creates a long-term reputation where respect will be theirs because they stood up for what was important to them during critical moments of personal decision.

 "I heard, Emily, that several people in your math class cheated on the last test and are now being disciplined. When I was at parent-teacher conference last night, your math teacher commented on your reputation for honesty and how he knows he can always trust you to do what is right."

Reading Habits

Often, especially during the teenage years, recreational reading goes by the wayside in favor of required reading for your children's school curriculum. Create an environment where your teenagers have the opportunity to continue to read for pleasure. Keep uplifting magazines and books accessible. As your children read what interests them, the habit of lifelong learning will be established, and the concepts learned during such reading will embed themselves in your children's minds. Sometimes, when you are sensitive to such opportunities, it might even be useful to allow your teenagers to be relieved of household duties in favor of finishing a good book.

> "Brian, I notice that you are almost finished with your book. I'll do your dishes tonight so you can have a half hour to just read and still have plenty of time for your homework. I loved that book too, and I know how hard it is to put down a book near the end."

(You probably taught your children how to serve when they were very young. Such service now by you, during opportune, unexpected moments, will be remembered and emulated as they mature.)

Social Skills

Being socially capable can be taught from the early years of your children's lives but becomes especially important as they desire to fit in and be accepted by their peers during their teenage years. Practice appropriate social responses and skills in the safe environment of your home so your children will be more apt to do the same in their own social circles.

Teach your children how to comfortably say hello to people they meet on the street, in the classroom, at work, or when shopping. This makes it much easier for them to be self-assured and fearless when they are stressed or trying to impress another person. They might even be willing to practice these skills in your presence. The goal is for them to be able to say hello and then ask two consecutive questions to get a conversation going. Often, especially with less confident children, role-playing is useful to get them into the mode and to understand the possibilities of conversation.

"I sense that you want to be able to say more to John than just hi when you pass him in the halls at school. Would you like me to show you how to start a conversation so you can be more comfortable if you happen to be in line with him during lunch?

"Okay. First, think of something he might know that you don't. For example, you said he is in your math class. You might ask him about the latest assignment and ask him if he understands the integer homework yet, because you don't quite get it.

"Or, you might make a comment about something you admire about him. You might ask him about practicing the trumpet, how long he has been doing it, and where he got his instrument.

"You want to practice with me? Okay, I'll be John and you walk up behind me and start a conversation. I'll purposefully not talk much (mostly because I'm shy, too), and let's see how it goes."

Your children will also benefit from remembering people's names. Like other skills, this one must be practiced until it becomes more natural. Help your child learn that after being introduced to someone for the first time, repeating that person's name several times while initially conversing with him or her will help the name stick in their own heads. Associating the name with something they are already comfortable with in their own life helps, too. Finally, writing down the person's name and contact information after the initial conversation will keep this knowledge close at hand when their memory fails them. These skills will not only help them remember names later, but it will make it easier to learn new names as their circle of friends grows to include new associates, fellow acquaintances, casual friends they pass in the halls, and important friendships they wish to nurture.

"Zach, you have said that remembering names is hard for you. May I help? I do three things to remember a person's name when I first meet them. First, I ask a question about the name to help me see their name in my mind. For instance, when I met one of Dad's new bosses, Jacob Hanson, last week at the office for the first time, I asked him if he spelled his name H-a-n-s-o-n or H-a-n-s-e-n. This helped me see the name in my mind. Then, second, I repeated Mr. Hanson's name several times during our introductions.

"If I remember right, I said, 'Mr. Hanson, tell me more about your chemical engineering work since you have moved to our city.' He replied, and then I said, 'It has been wonderful to meet you, Mr. Hanson. I hope I can get to know your wife better. I will look for her at the Chemical Engineering wives' social this month.' Lastly, when it was time for me to leave, I said, 'Mr. Hanson, with an "o", it was my pleasure to meet you.' He smiled at me, and by that time, Zach, it was easy for me to associate Mr. Hanson's name with his face. Then, because this person is so important in Dad's career, I came home and added Mr. Jacob Hanson (with an 'o') to my address list along with his wife's name, which is Susan. I remember her name, because when he said it, I responded, 'Oh, that is the name of one of my sisters.'

"See, Zach, learning names is a skill just like any other social skill. Now, I know you feel out of place at this new high school, but I also know there is one certain girl whose name you would like to know. You'll be glad when you find it out, know how it is spelled, and can ask her a few questions to get a conversation started. Good luck!"

Children will also need schooling on table manners and eating habits. This will reflect their training clearly when they are in important social settings. You might ask yourself these questions:

Do your children eat with their mouths closed, wait to speak until they have swallowed, say "thank you" at the end of the meal, and ask to be excused from the table when finished? As a parent, you will probably do well to have an occasional, more formal meal where you teach these skills. It will be best received by your children just before an important prom date where they will be eating out at a more expensive restaurant. They will want to know which fork, knife, and spoon to pick up and when.

If you are uncomfortable with the etiquette required for such an occasional, educate yourself first and then offer to teach them. You don't need to necessarily demand such habits all of the time, but working to develop them at formal family meals will give your young people confidence when they want to impress a date or a potential employer, or simply want to feel confident in a social gathering.

As you give your children training in table manners, you may want to help them know how to handle awkward situations. What should they do with food that they can't chew? What should they do if they drop their silverware, tip over their water glass, or get sauce on their clothes? It is easier to talk it through and train them now than to have your teenagers turn into horrified basket cases because they don't know how to deal with a challenging situation when it arises on an important date.

Budgeting Skills

Budgeting skills are essential for the success of all young people preparing to leave the home. It is always easier to train children when they are younger. A twelve-year-old beginning to earn money by mowing the neighbor's lawn will be more likely to respond to training by his parents about handling his finances well than will a sixteen-year-old who has been working for several years and has spent her money with little thought of future obligations and needs.

Shopping Skills

During the teenage years, your children should learn to occasionally buy enough food to last for a week of cooking for themselves. Shopping may seem like torture to some, but it is easier to help them learn to shop wisely, cook well, and feed themselves nutritionally now than to have them become sick or unhealthy, use up all their money on fast food, and face total frustration during the first months of their complete independence.

Help them learn that some foods can be eaten "as is," such as peanut butter, raisins, oatmeal, canned meats, canned pork and beans, and canned soups. This can provide the staples for their menus and aid in shorter, easier meal preparation times. Fresh, perishable foods and frozen staples can then fill out the menu and add nutrition.

Cooking Skills

I have found that the best time to teach cooking skills to young people is usually during the summertime through their younger teenage years and then on the weekends as they grow older. Knowing how to prepare basic foods will enable them to cook independently as they make family meals and will give them confidence when they are completely on their own.

Possible practice cooking sessions might include such items as rice, macaroni, spaghetti, noodles, potatoes (which can be baked in the microwave or prepared easily from dehydrated potatoes), meats, fish, and eggs.

Foods they should learn to cook in a fry pan or on a griddle are pancakes, French toast, fried and scrambled eggs, and different kinds of meats. They need to know how to assemble a sandwich. (I can hear some of you laughing at me now, but I work with so many young people who are clueless about how to prepare these kinds of foods and instead head to the local fast food restaurant to eat. If your children can learn basic food preparation skills they can save themselves a lot of money and be able to eat on their own schedule.) As part of this preparation, make sure all your family members are aware of how to prepare and store food safely to prevent botulism or food poisoning.

While these are not the only habits necessary for young people twelve to eighteen years of age, they prove a good foundation for any and all other skills you deem useful to their independence. Be diligent, observe where they are lacking knowledge and skill, and (as much as they will allow) continue to teach and train until the last day before they are off and gone.

PART THREE: *Show Them*

CHAPTER TEN

Delegate Household Jobs

As you desire to increase your children's capacity to do household jobs on a day-to-day basis, you will probably want to oversee a little bit less yourself in order to allow your children more self-initiative. Continually taking responsibility for what your children do on a weekly or daily basis and telling them what to do tonight, this afternoon, and even before dinner give children more frequent opportunities to complain and whine. "Mom, why are you making me do that job again? Don't you remember, you just had me do it three days ago and it's Jordan's turn now? I don't like to do that job anyway and it isn't fair!"

I have found it is best to delegate household jobs on more of a long-term basis. You decide what needs to be done, how often it needs to be done, who in your family would be good candidates for completing each job, and then set the schedule for a few months or longer. This allows your children to "own" a job for a reasonable period of time and get faster and better at it, and it also makes it easier for you to remember who is helping where.

The standards for various jobs should be clearly delineated, usually in writing, to reduce the amount of time you spend overseeing the job completion after you have trained your children how to do the job. The Standards charts (see pages 40–47) allow your children to be more independent, give them a written standard to comply with, and allow you to have written standards for the job when it comes time to clarify and correct.

This concept of delineating the jobs, detailing the specifics for them to be completed correctly, and then delegating them to various family members is extremely critical when both parents are working or there is a single parent running the home. Nothing pulls children to feel responsibility like a frank discussion of what needs to be done for the home to run smoothly, a further explanation of standards that are to be met, along with a timetable for job completion, and then an invitation to choose what they would be willing to do.

Decide with your children how long they will have a particular job before you make changes. This allows children and parents to settle into a routine and to know, for example, that the current job arrangements "will last until the end of the summer, at which time we will redo the job responsibilities for the new school year."

Once these items have been decided upon, continue the discussion with ideas about how to deal with unknowns that come up unexpectedly.

 "Chris, I really appreciate all you do to help around the house, especially when I'm still at work. Now that Dad isn't here anymore, we'll both have to increase the amount of work we do around the house and yard to keep them up. Thanks for accepting responsibility for half of the jobs we talked about last week.

"Now, things will always come up that we can't anticipate. Sometimes it will be me that needs your help. Sometimes it will be you that needs my help. What will be the best way for us to work together when the unexpected knocks at our door?

"For example, I have a meeting tonight and I can't do the dishes as I have committed to do. Is there some job I can exchange with you so the dishes will get done?"

Work toward Self-judgment

Let your children use the Standards charts to check off the standards as they meet them. Use the job charts or personalized index cards you or your children have prepared to check off the children's jobs as they do them. After training them, and as you become more and more confident that your children are reliable, let them judge themselves the quality to which they finish these jobs (unless you find that they don't keep their word or don't work to the standards you have commonly set). If it is appropriate and you make the decision to do so, you could begin paying them for some of their house and yard work.

With teenage children you might let them figure how much pay they should be getting each week and submit an invoice to you, maybe on Saturday morning. You might find it useful to give a bonus for basic household jobs completed without reminding (meaning they used their self-initiative) and jobs done to an extra level of excellence. On the other hand, you might also determine what deductions will be made for jobs not completed in a timely manner, jobs you had to nag about, and jobs that were not done properly.

Let your children grow up as fast as they can in this area of their lives even as you allow them some leeway in other areas of recreation and fun. As they become competent, show appreciation for their work ethic. Making a formal payment arrangement between parents and children can greatly benefit your family.

Look at your own family situation and alter, upgrade, or change the way you work with your children and teenagers to have more productive job delegation, meet the standards of excellence you desire for housework, and help them discover and use their self-initiative, even as you choose how and when to pay them.

Allowance

I'm often asked what I feel about allowances and paying children to work. It has been my experience that every person who lives in a home should have some responsibilities that "pay" for their living there. In other words, some household jobs are "your responsibility" simply because "you live here." These are the fundamental chores that all family members do to contribute to the well-being of the whole family. There is no payment for these jobs because everyone helps with the running of the home.

If not giving your children an allowance suits your family's situation, you might like to offer some moneymaking opportunities for your children. Miscellaneous jobs can be designated that allow children to work for money, but only after their own jobs have been completed successfully. These might be more complex, difficult, or even tedious jobs that are often left undone. Or they could be simple ones like digging dandelions from the lawn or picking up rocks in the garden. These additional jobs can have a direct dollar amount value. This gives children incentive to do additional chores beyond their regular responsibilities that can be valued in real cash. Make sure the jobs the children do are reviewed as soon as possible and that the children receive payment promptly. This reduces misunderstanding between parents and children. It also keeps a direct association in your children's minds between what they do and what they earn.

"Heather, I will be happy to pay you for weeding the side yard of those thorny weeds. I will pay ten cents each, but you have to pull them close to the ground so the root comes up, too. Put them in stacks of twenty-five weeds each, and I'll come when you are done. We'll count them together, and I'll pay you in cash. You will have about two hours before dinner tonight and some more time tomorrow night to help you earn money for the weekend movie with your friends."

The question of whether or not to give children an allowance has caused some warm discussions in many homes. If you decide to also give your children an allowance (which by definition is cash out of your hands with no effort at their end), you should probably consider identifying with your children what they will be responsible to purchase on their own.

"We are going to begin giving you an allowance each week. This will allow you to have some money so you can start paying tithing, and then go to the movies, get a treat at the mall, or buy something for yourself occasionally. However, we also feel that it would be good for you to be in charge of buying some of your own items now, too. You'll have to learn to save part of your money for your own purchases. Would you be willing to buy your own socks from your allowance? We figure if you save about 25 percent of your allowance, you will have enough to buy these items once in a while."

As children grow older, the allowance might increase along with the responsibility to purchase such items as shampoo, hair products, makeup, and eventually clothing and shoes. This practice of increasing their allowances might continue until your children are given more substantial amounts, but they should also be encouraged to independently provide for up to half of their own personal needs.

Remember, help your children realize that some work is done without pay, some work can be done for pay, and that financial gain always brings financial responsibilities. Thus your children will be well-prepared for eventual financial independence and success. (See more about finances in chapter 23.)

CHAPTER ELEVEN

Finish What You Start

Making decisions as a family about "finishing" can take a lot of stress out of life. It is a fundamental skill when training children to work. Initially, you will want to work on four "how to finish" skills: how to finish in the bathroom, how to finish the dishes, how to finish playing, and how to finish the day.

As you train your children in age-specific chores, you are also teaching them principles that will enhance their individual performance and make everyone's life easier. Because one of these skills is the ability to finish, when you teach your family members how to finish household tasks, you make everyone's life easier.

Finish in the Bathroom

I suggest you begin the finishing training process in the bathroom because it is a commonly used room, and everyone benefits from a tidy bathroom. Teach all family members three finishing skills when they use this room.

Teeth. First, after family members brush their teeth properly, they should put their toothbrush and the toothpaste away appropriately and wash their spittle down the sink.

Toilet. Second, all family members should flush the toilet after they use it, put down the toilet lid, and check that enough toilet paper is available for the next person. Show how to replace the toilet paper roll and put the almost-used-up roll on top of the new roll to make it convenient for the next person. Older family members should know where extra toilet paper is stored in the house so that they can replenish the bathroom once the last full roll of toilet paper is taken out of the cupboard.

Towels. Third, all family members should hang up bath towels neatly after they bathe or shower, open the shower curtain or door to air out the room, and make sure the bathroom is in better shape when they leave than when they entered.

At the age-appropriate time, family members should learn and practice all of the above techniques, with adequate supervision, lots of positive acknowledgment and compliments for jobs well done, and maybe even treats for good performance.

After several days of practice (for some families, it might take several weeks), you will notice an increased willingness on each family member's part to keep the bathroom clean. You may even find you have a "sheriff" or two who will want to help others do their part, too.

When family members are successful in these three simple bathroom-finishing tasks, a parent's responsibilities are lessened to a great degree. Each new skill that is taught and then becomes part of a family's routine means less stress for those who are trying to help children grow up to be competent adults.

Finish the Dishes

Another finishing task to be learned is how to finish the dishes. If your family sits down together for a meal, set these standards for everyone in your family when the meal is completed:

1. All family members are to ask a parent if they may be excused from the table.

2. All remove their own dishes from the table, scrape any leftover food remnants into the trash, and put the dishes in the sink or dishwasher.

3. All take one or more other items from the table to put away, such as salt and pepper, napkin holder, condiments, jam or jelly, and so on.

4. All push in their own chairs.

If everyone in the family has these four responsibilities, the family members in charge of "finishing" the dishes will have a much easier time getting their job done.

Finishing the dishes really begins when the cooks enter the kitchen. Teach your children, when they are your kitchen helpers, to fill the sink with hot, soapy water. This will provide an easy place to rinse preparation tools and containers while the meal is being prepared. It will also provide a place for pans and baking dishes to soak during the meal.

Final finishing is done after the meal. All members of the family should participate at least once a week in meal cleanup. Sometimes it will be necessary to have them participate more often so no one is left alone doing dishes at the end of the family meal. Then the process will become faster and much easier. Usually one mature family member stays in the kitchen with the helpers until the work is done. Family dishwashing "finishing" standards can be decided upon, written up, laminated, and posted in the kitchen.

For instance, you might consider having a chart like the example on page 105.

Choose consistent standards and insist that everyone follows through. Sometimes you may have to hire a "family sheriff" to conduct inspections and give a sign-off. Whatever your method, ask for all family members' help, let everyone have an opportunity to participate, and make sure that "finishing" standards are kept.

If you can get dishwashing done right and in a timely manner, then each and every day's work will be a bit lighter and easier for all family members.

Finish Playtime

One way to have children clean up toys, a project, or a game is to tell them it is spic-and-span time. Give children a five-minute warning so they can wrap up whatever scenarios they are working through. Then encourage them to begin a cleanup session. After the mess is cleared properly and has been inspected, it is useful to "pay" the children for their help and obedience. You might have them choose a treat from your Spic-and-Span jar. This is a special place where you keep small snacks for their enjoyment and motivation. The treats might be small toys, food snacks, or slips of paper with a "time" treat (for example, reading a book aloud or playing with them for five minutes). Of course, washing their hands will need to be part of the cleanup if food is used as a treat. This method of encouraging cleaning up is especially effective when their friends are present, for soon all of the children will clean up on their own initiative just for the upcoming treat.

Finish the Day

Children need to contribute to finishing the day. Encourage your children to pick up all their personal belongings and put them away

Finishing the dishes means . . .

- ☐ The table is cleared and wiped clean

- ☐ The chairs are neatly in their places

- ☐ The dishes are started in the dishwasher (or washed, rinsed, dried, and put away by hand)

- ☐ The counters are wiped clean

- ☐ The stove and burners are wiped clean

- ☐ The sink is scrubbed

- ☐ The taps are shined

- ☐ All cooking supplies are put away

- ☐ All leftover food is covered and stored in the refrigerator

- ☐ The floor is swept

before they retire. If they do not, a fun way to give incentive for this habit is the Buy-It-Back box.

The Buy-It-Back box holds any toys or personal items that were not put away at the end of the day. A parent puts the items in a box, and the only way they can be retrieved is for the child to do an extra chore, such as walk the dog around the block twice or take care of the baby for twenty minutes. Or children could buy back their items by picking up one toy that is lying around for each year of their age. Or, if you have a yard to maintain, they could pick up rocks or fallen apples or pull off spent flowers.

The system also works in reverse. When children pick up after the adults, the parents earn back their items by pushing the children on the swings, taking them for a walk, or reading to them.

"Yes, Kelsey, your play shoes ended up in the Buy-It-Back box last night. I asked you to pick them up on your way to bed, but I found them later in the family room. Because you are ten years old and there were two shoes, you can earn them back by picking up twenty fist-sized rocks from the area we are getting ready to plant with lawn. Put the rocks in a bucket and leave it next to the garbage can."

Finishing a task—whether it be in the bathroom, after a meal, when playtime is done, or at the end of the day—will help return the home to order and instill useful lifelong habits in children.

CHAPTER TWELVE

Job Training the Right Way

In addition to the many facets of training that have already been discussed, it will be useful to understand several further concepts to truly find success as you train your children.

The Moment of "Abandonment"

There will come a critical moment after training is complete when your children become competent to do a quality job and are able to finish completely. At this point, it is necessary to leave the children to do the job alone.

Before you do so, talk to your children about the feeling of "abandonment" that they may experience. Explain to them how important it is to you that they have learned the skills you have discussed and practiced. Help them understand that they may feel strange having to do their jobs alone without supervision. Help them know beforehand what they might feel and then discuss how they feel after they have had this experience for the first time. This is extremely important.

"David, you are now ready to be left alone to do the job. You won't need me to watch over you anymore.

"You might feel lonely when I'm not by you all the time, but I know you'll do the job just like we practiced.

"I will come when you are finished and we will check to make sure you have done everything right. And we will talk about how it felt to be mature enough not to need me watching you work all the time."

If you pay careful attention to your children during this critical moment when they move from your supervision to self-supervision, you will save yourself many challenges later. It is always better to talk with children in advance about how they might feel than to have to deal with it later.

Reliability

As you help your children move to this new position of self-responsibility, speak to them about being reliable regarding the important chores that are their responsibilities. When children know what is expected, have received a written set of standards detailing the job, and know when they will be "finished" with this job to meet your criteria, you can introduce the concept of reliability.

 "Scott, I'm so glad that you now know how to clean up your bedroom every morning. You open the curtains, make your bed, and shut your closet door after dressing. I've been here every morning during this first week of school to help you. You have done these jobs through the weekend without me watching.

"It's so nice to think how much I will soon be able to rely on you. I'm glad you have committed to show me how reliable you are this next week. Now I know I will be able to trust you to do this job the right way, all the way to the end, and then come and tell me when it is finished.

"If you want me to come and inspect it, I will. But knowing you, I suspect that after a couple of days, I can rely on you to do the job without inspection. When I come to your room later in the day, I know I'll be delighted because it will be neat and clean just as you have done all the other days while you were learning how to do it."

Long-term Supervision

Although there may be a long period of time when you will feel you are micro-managing children as they learn the desired skills, it is important that you eventually move away and let them exercise their independency muscles. This is difficult and yet very necessary. Usually parents make the mistake, when they do decide to let go, of letting go so completely that the children feel less and less responsibility to finish their jobs. Some parents abandon their supervisory duty altogether, and children learn quickly that they can get by with less than a quality job and with less frequency, and so the whole training falls apart.

Many parents have said to me, "We did fine for a while, but then I stopped following up and they stopped doing. Now, I just do it myself because it is faster than hassling them to do their jobs."

Everything that has been worked on can come unraveled so easily. As a parent you must not let this happen. You must supervise, correct, and compliment again and again and again. You must follow through. If your son flits off to Saturday morning baseball practice and you know full well he had time to make his bed and chose not to do so, you must take action.

One wise mother packed her younger children into the car, drove to the park, found her son, quietly explained that his bed hadn't been made, drove him home, waited in the running car while he made his bed, and then drove him back to his activity. She got little else done that morning, but her son learned (as did all the other family members in the car) that Mom means business when she asks you do to a job. This particular son was careful to make his bed and straighten his room every morning from that day on. His mother cared enough to teach him, to train him, and then to follow up to keep him responsible for his particular chores.

Not every parent has the luxury and time to trot off to the park to get their children and bring them home just for bed making. In the case of working parents, this might best be handled after you have returned from work. Sometimes making the bed at 4 P.M. is just as effective a discipline measure as getting brought home from play, especially if a second infraction brings additional discipline, perhaps the loss of dessert at dinner.

Help Them Keep Commitments

Children and teenagers all know how to extend the boundaries of your patience. They will commit to come home at 4 P.M. so they can practice the piano before dinner and then call to ask (because they are having such a fun time) if they can practice after dinner. Well, you know what will probably happen if you let them stay longer. The practicing won't get done.

Your teenager might ask to do his chores after he has gone with friends to the tennis tournament because he forgot to arrange for someone else in the family to do them. Because the tournament lasts all day, those chores will likely remain undone if you consent.

Your younger children might say, "Please, just this time," "Can't we?" and "Why not?" enough to drive you wild with indecision and guilt.

So, as you approach parenting and training your children to work, decide to decide. What will be your regular standard for helping them keep their commitments? Will you allow certain exceptions and, if so, when will you allow them? Can you be firm and not give in to whining, manipulation, and sulking?

Being a parent is a very difficult occupation. Somehow, it seems you are always working with family members who are one step ahead of you and who are more determined than you are. But if you have rules, standards, and some routine to this season of your life, you should also have a set way of handling situations when the chores have been left undone because the family member is away, the teenager wants to play first and then work, and younger children poke and pull at your indecisiveness until you want to surrender.

Sit down with your family and decide how you will work things out when one child wants to stay longer at a friend's and will miss setting the dinner table, when a teenager will be gone on his day to prepare dinner, and when another child has asked to stay late for a movie at a friend's home when it's her responsibility to feed the dogs.

It will make for a more wonderful, unified family life when everyone knows the rules and you are confident in enforcing them. It is all right to say,

"No, not this time. You didn't make previous arrangements. Come home tonight and next time let's plan ahead better."

When Your Children Fail You Again and Again

For various reasons, some children, even with thorough training, plenty of compliments, lots of attention, and careful supervision, seem to thrive on disobedience and a lack of exuberance about doing their household responsibilities. For some children this will be a temporary situation and for others it will be a lifelong challenge.

For the occasional slackers, try to understand what they feel and why they feel it. It might mean sitting next to them and sympathizing with them.

 "Yes, Alex, I can see you feel it is hard to sweep the floor. Yes, I know that your friends don't have to work like this. I know that Trent sometimes even makes fun of you because you can't play until your chores are done.

"Alex, let's just sit here together and do nothing for a bit. When you feel ready to go again and get this floor swept so you can run outside and play, I'll get up, too, and go back to washing the dishes."

Alex, of course, will appreciate the attention and after a moment or two of continued complaining, will often get up and get going. After all, his friends are waiting.

It is important that you don't give in to complaining, don't give too many exceptions to your stated rules, and don't waffle. Your children have jobs, they can do them, and they should do them. Encourage them, love them, let them explain their feelings, and then help them see that as soon as their jobs are done, they can go on to other, more fun activities.

For the chronic slackers, there is usually a different problem. It may be that they are among the younger children and feel they don't match up to the speed and agility of their siblings. It may be they feel they carry an unfair load of the work. It could be any number of causes, so it is important to try and see past the whining, complaining, and slacking to the real problem.

One wise father realized that his youngest son did have a point. He was doing the grunt household jobs because the other siblings were older and more capable of complex jobs. This seemed demeaning to him. The father asked his son which of the complex, "big-boy" jobs he would like to learn to do. When the son indicated that he felt he could start the dishwasher as well as any of the older children, the father taught him how to load the dishwasher, how to add soap, lock the lid, and start the machine. Then he let this youngest son have that job for a week's training to see if he could be competent and reliable. In the meantime, an older son agreed to take on one of the "grunt" jobs the youngest sibling had been doing (actually he was pleased to get by with less work). It was a win-win situation for all parties and the chronic complainer found new confidence and felt that he was being treated equally.

The Whining Child

Some children seem to thrive on whining. Move this habit out of your children's repertoire as soon as possible. Whining is a most disagreeable interaction to watch, whether in public or private, and it shouldn't be tolerated.

But how do you help children stop whining? There are several methods, one of which seems to work quite well. It is practiced in private, usually when the child is home.

"Lara, I hear you whining. When you can tell me what is on your mind with your big-girl voice, I will be happy to listen.

Until then my earflaps are folded . . . Oh, would you like to try again?"

In other words, the parent refuses to interact with the child when the child is whining.

 "Yes, Lara, I can hear you, but you are still using your whining voice. This is how a grown-up talks . . . Would you like to try it again?

"No? I'll be in the family room dusting when you want to talk to me like a big girl."

It is important that both parents firmly continue to stop interacting with children when they are in whine mode. Simply say you will talk, listen, and respond only when they speak to you with a mature voice.

 "I'm sorry, Lara, but that is still not an acceptable voice. Let me demonstrate. We talk like this when we want to explain our problems. Now you can try it again."

Motivational Aids

Parents would be wise, especially with younger children, to provide a visual aid to help children see their progress and their accomplishments and to remind them of their jobs. After the Training Children to Work Master Plan is in place, stickers on charts, colored-in graphs, or any other measuring tool that indicates to your children that they are improving will provide greater motivation. You may also want to associate certain jobs with certain treats. A well-made bed gets a big tickle-time, the dishes done right and in a timely manner merits reading with Mom for ten minutes, and hanging up a towel after bathing is good for a bit of perfumed lotion for the girls and a splash of aftershave for the boys.

Children will probably get bored with charts and graphs if two additional elements are not present. There need to be both well-clarified goals and significant rewards.

"Daniel, this week we are working on making your bed in the morning. You have three other jobs during the day, too. I have made up a chart to show your jobs and you can add one gold star each time I have inspected your work and passed you off. Seven stars are good for a treat from the candy jar. If you get twenty-eight stars, or do all your four jobs for a full week, you get a trip out with Dad for ice cream."

Also, parents need to be sensitive to children needing to move from one set of jobs to another as they mature, have a birthday, or get bored with the current motivational system. You might remove jobs from the chart that they are regularly doing well and add new ones.

"Madison, you have made your bed and done your other three jobs for a full month. Wow, you have also gone with Dad four times to get ice cream! Now it is time to take those jobs off the chart and give you a few new ones! Would you be willing to empty the silverware holder in the dishwasher in the morning and put it away? We will make this a new entry on your job chart.

"We aren't going to keep adding stars for the jobs you do well. They are part of your personal habits now. But if you keep doing your four jobs and also do this new one each day, we will add one star for your four jobs and another one for the new job you are training to do. Again, seven stars are good for a candy treat and fourteen stars, or doing all your previous jobs and also the new ones, will mean another trip with Dad for ice cream."

Even with charts and index card boxes in place, children enjoy other motivators to keep it lively and interesting. A timer is one motivator.

"Emily, can you get your job done in ten minutes and receive a chocolate chip treat? How about if we make this job worth ten chocolate chips? Every minute past ten minutes it takes you to finish the job, we will take away one chocolate chip, and for every minute faster you are we will add one chip."

Or how about using the clock as a motivator?

"Nathan, can you get the dishes done before the clock shows 1:11? That will mean you have ten minutes to do a great job. I'll even throw in a bonus sticker if you don't complain and finish up before that clock says 1:11."

Or how about connecting a cleanup job with an upcoming event?

"Dad has just called. Do you think we can pick up the toys in the family room before he walks in the door from work? If you can, I'll let you fill in another square on your graph! Yes, Marci, you can help, too. I'll even pick up ten toys to help you get a good start. Ready? Let's get started!"

Organization Party

As much as possible, use your imagination to make it fun to live in your house. Make it worthwhile to cooperate and beneficial to help out. Use your imagination to reduce the length of cleanup time. For example, cleaning up small items such as Legos, blocks, marbles, and action figure or doll accessories will be less burdensome if they are collected in a large, clear jar kept conveniently in the kitchen cupboard instead of putting them back every day into their respective containers. When the toy collection jar is full, have an "organization party" and organize these smaller toy pieces into muffin tins with the children and then let them help put the toy pieces back where they belong. When the organizing is done, give each cooperative child a treat for partici-pating in the party—and a chance to divide between themselves all the pennies, nickels, and dimes that have been collected!

CHAPTER THIRTEEN

Moving from Yes/No Choices to Yes/Yes Choices

Viewing children as adults in smaller bodies gives you the opportunity to treat them with greater respect and to gain their esteem in return. This is a great improvement over talking down to them, which causes resentment and often defiant disobedience. When you talk to them as equals, they are more likely to respond with interest in obedience and compliance.

Telling children what to do creates challenge and conflict. When we say, "Justin, put your shoes in the basket," or "Cory, go clean your room," or "Rachael, come wash the dishes," it is like your spouse telling you what to do with superiority and authority in his or her voice. It just doesn't sit well.

Indicate Expectations

However, children respond quite readily when they are talked to "adult to adult." This is best accomplished by focusing on what needs to be done, not on who is to do the job. In other words, saying *what* needs to be done can help all your interactions with your children move to a healthier level.

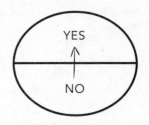 "Justin, shoes belong in the basket after we come in the house."

"Cory, when we had family council on Sunday you committed to clean your room before dinner tonight. Dinner is in the oven and the room needs to be cleaned now."

"Rachael, your job is to wash the dishes tonight. The dishes are awaiting your attention."

In other words, it is better to say what needs to be done instead of telling children what to do. The decision is left to the children, but the parent has clearly stated the desired results.

Offer Choices

Children appreciate having choices. Too many choices can be confusing, but simple choices are essential to their growth and personal discipline. You encourage obedience by the way you offer choices to your children. "Cory, your bedroom is dirty and needs cleaning," leaves two choices for Cory: I will or I will not clean up my room.

However, you can quickly move children from whether or not they will obey to *how* they will obey by offering two "yes" choices. This encourages obedience and yet still leaves freedom of choice to children.

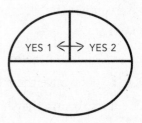

"Cory, your bedroom needs cleaning before dinner. Would you rather start by making your bed or picking up your dirty clothes?"

You have still offered choices, but you are moving the child from whether or not he will obey to a readiness to obey by offering him the choice of what to do first. This way of encouraging obedience, especially when you watch until they obey, and follow up with objective compliments, molds and shapes a character of discipline.

Move to Action

For reluctant children, additional motivation may be needed. It is now time to move the children to "action."

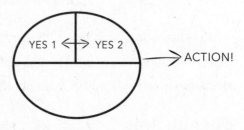

"Cory, you have chosen to make your bed first. That is a great way to start! How long do you think it will take? Twenty seconds? How about if I turn my back and begin to count and you can tell me when you are done. Let's see just how long it really does take."

When children have complied with the needed action, objective compliments help to cement their desire to please, and eventually they will be obedient without hesitation.

"Cory, I see your bed neatly made with the bedspread smoothed and the pillow tucked nicely at the head of the bed."

Objective praise cannot be refuted or denied, and children can remember the pleasant feeling of praise from someone they desire to please.

Children need to know that not only will you tell them what needs to be done, give them choices, and compliment them, but also that you will make sure they have completed what you have stated needs doing. At the beginning of training a child, this means watching until you are obeyed. Later, when the child has shown that he can be counted on to obey without watching, he can come back to you and report that he has accomplished the desired task. At this point, an inspection may be done and compliments readily handed out.

Come Back and Report

Eventually, the child can be trusted to be obedient and do a reasonable job and, when returning and reporting, may receive a compliment without inspection.

> "Cory, how pleasant it is to know that when I walk down the hall when I'm done with the dishes, your bed will be made and I can smile inside."

This is a marvelous time for both child and parent, because the mutual relationship has reached a point of great trust.

Of course, a mother or father cannot spend their whole lives watching children make their beds or do other chores, but during the training period the following elements are important:

- State what needs to be done.
- Offer two "yes" choices to encourage obedience.
- Motivate children to action by treats, timers, a game, or even a competition.
- Wait and watch until you are obeyed.
- Objectively compliment the accomplishments of the child.

Limit Their Choices

Giving choices increases success in your interactions with your children, but too many choices can be confusing and frustrating.

When you work with children, especially younger ones, help them maintain their dignity and independence by giving them choices they can comprehend and appreciate. At the same time, limit the choices so they feel safe in their response, knowing they have "given the right answer" and are pleasing you.

If you offer too many choices, you give too much latitude for noncompliance because the child becomes uncomfortable and moves more easily toward defiance. For instance, "It's time to set the table. When would you like to begin?" is full of too many choices. The options are left wide open and may lead to the response, "I don't want to do it. Not now, not later, not ever. And you can't make me."

On the other hand, if you approach the same situation with fewer choices, success is likely to follow.

> "It's time to set the table now. Would you like to put on the forks or spoons first?"

Stating what needs to be done, and when, establishes the "timing" and thus eliminates that choice. Offering several choices within the parameters of "it's time to set the table now" helps children move from whether or not they will comply to which of the choices within compliance they would prefer.

The importance of working with children using a firm but gentle tone while offering simple choices will increase motivation, completion of their tasks, and a desire to please. If you are loose, nonspecific, and vague, you will find yourself frustrated with the results. "It's time to get ready for bed" is a statement so broad and with so many choices, it is unlikely you will get anyone to bed anytime soon. On the other hand, if you are firm and specific you will have more success.

> "It's eight o'clock and time to prepare for bed. Shall we begin right this minute or shall we begin after I have tried to say the alphabet backward?"

If you say, "Your towel is on the bathroom floor. Make sure to pick it up before you run outside to play," you have given too many choices—do it now, do it later, or don't do it at all and hope Mom won't remember until later. This range of choices is too broad for the child.

Instead, use specific comments and questions to stay in control.

"I see that you haven't picked up your towel in the bathroom. Would you like me to watch you do it or stand in the doorway with my back turned and then inspect afterward?"

As you go about your interactions with your children, look for ways to interact with those you nurture with specific instructions and a choice or two, but don't give too much leeway. Success will follow as you take charge, offer some choices, and expect to be obeyed.

Parenting, nurturing, and teaching are hard. But, oh, what joy you will experience when they begin to respond to your requests with desire and obedience!

CHAPTER FOURTEEN

Self-initiative: The End Goal

You want to help mold your sometimes self-centered, whining children into independent, hardworking, and capable adults. This happens best when you teach your children how to work, when to work, and what steps to take toward being self-initiating in their work. Let's suppose it is the start of a new school year, and you have decided it is time for important changes. Each member of your family will be given one small morning job, a short evening job, and several household chores on Saturday to complete. After a period of training, let's suppose you plan to move your children toward successful completion of their work without their being asked, prodded, or reminded. This will allow household jobs to be shared among all family members with the possibility of competent completion. (And, of course, your long-term plans include more complete training during the summer months.)

There are four important concepts to consider as you approach training your family members how to work independently.

1. Clarify with your family what jobs need to be done for the household to run smoothly, which of these many jobs they will have an

opportunity to complete on a daily basis in the morning and in the evening, and which will be their responsibilities on Saturday. All children and teenagers need to have household jobs because anyone who lives in a home should participate in maintaining it. You need to hold everyone responsible to contribute regularly. Initially, choose the simple but repetitive jobs they can do to make the load lighter for maintaining the home, cleaning the yard, and keeping up with the laundry.

"Anna and Luke, things are going to be a bit different from now on with me going back to work. There are six morning jobs we need to have done before we leave for work and school. They include cleaning our own bedrooms (opening the curtains, making the bed, and cleaning up the room). We also need to empty the dishwasher, put a batch of wash in, and empty the kitchen wastebasket. I propose that I handle getting the laundry started, we all take care of our own bedrooms, and that we draw straws for which of you will empty the dishwasher and which will empty the kitchen wastebasket. Let's plan to keep these jobs throughout the school year because then each day everyone will know who does what and with practice we can get better and better at our work. On Saturday we will need to clean the whole house together. Let's talk about how to divide up that work so we will have everything in place for this weekend."

2. After jobs have been chosen or assigned, teach each individual how to do the jobs to an acceptable standard of quality. Take plenty of time to teach them the right way to do each job. It is useful to have written Standards charts so everyone can be easily reminded of the expectations needed to complete the job right (see pages 40–47). Laminating

the job charts and storing them right in the room to be cleaned will make everyone's life easier.

> "Chris, remember you will be in charge of straightening the main bathroom each morning. This will include cleaning out the sink, wiping down the toilet seat, and emptying the wastebasket. Your evening job will be to clear and wipe the table after dinner. On Saturday you will be in charge of cleaning your half of the bedroom, deep cleaning the main bathroom, and sweeping the front porch."

3. Work with family members and a timer to show them that with some diligence they can get better each and every time they do their chores. While this part of the training takes a considerable amount of encouragement and patience, once children and teenagers become competent at their work, they are more likely to comprehend that repetition makes it easier and getting the job done means more free time at the other end of their day.

4. Incorporate the concept of self-initiative, one of the most important principles a young child, a teenager, or even an adult learns. There is great satisfaction in doing a job well, doing it completely, and doing it without being asked. Reward your family members generously for any self-initiative that is shown as they work on their jobs.

For example, you might use colored drinking glasses at dinner for those members of your family who did something during the day using their self-initiative. These colored drinking glasses became a symbol of their achievements and their willingness to cooperate.

> "Melissa, you get to have a gold glass at dinner tonight because I didn't have to remind you to dust the front room this morning. David, you get a gold glass, too, because I noticed that

you made your bed and cleaned up your room before breakfast without me saying anything."

"Aaron, you can have a gold glass tomorrow night for dinner if you will do one of your jobs tonight or tomorrow without me reminding you that it needs doing."

Take the time to clarify for your children how they can best help out at home, teach them the methods for successfully doing their jobs, time your children so they become more competent at their chores, and, finally, introduce the concept of self-initiation, so they do assigned responsibilities on their own without being asked.

PART FOUR: *Nurture Them*

CHAPTER FIFTEEN

Become Insistent, Consistent, and Persistent

From the moment children are born, parents are influencing those children's behaviors. Your interactions, moods, and responses all affect your children's lives, their sense of well-being, and their ability to respond appropriately to life's many experiences.

As you begin to say "no" to children, tell them they must wait, or remove them quickly and dramatically from unsafe situations, you are influencing your children's future reactions to those same circumstances.

Confusion sets in when parents are firm one time and then lax the next, when they are warm and concerned when the first situation arises and then are cold or angry when the situation repeats itself. There are several basic parental personality traits that bring children security, safety, and stability. These are the important first steps to successful parenting. These traits include being insistent, consistent, and persistent when it comes to obedience. Or in other words, do they know you expect to be obeyed every time? And once they know, do you follow through to make sure that they do exactly as you have asked?

Being Insistent

A parent must insist on being obeyed completely and in a timely manner. For example, if you tell children that it is time to put down their toys and picture books and put on their shoes, you must make it desirable for them to obey. If you state a specific need, it is your duty as a parent to see that your children obey as directed. There will be times when it can be done a little later, when it can be done in a different way than before, and even times when it can be done with a little flair. But pity the parent who doesn't follow through, the parent who doesn't insist on obedience. How quickly children learn that sulking, postponing, and defying are effective ways to resist obedience and the completion of their responsibilities.

A parent who understands that nurturing power lies in being insistent knows that being a parent means being a parent all the time—especially when it is inconvenient or the timing doesn't allow for thorough discipline. If you have said that the book needs to be put down and the shoes put on, make sure that the children—especially the children who are not used to you being insistent—are watched carefully until they completely obey.

First, indicate the desired behavior:

> "Brad, it is time for the book to be closed and put on the shelf. Then both shoes need to be on your feet so you can walk to school."

Next, wait and watch until you are obeyed. When training children, a parent must be unrelentingly clear to the end of the stated need: the book should be put away and the shoes put on.

Most parents have experiences with children who are resistant to obedience, prefer play to work, and even sass occasionally. Such children need an insistent parent to make sure that they know the rules, are capable of keeping them, and are encouraged with extra attention to move along and get the assigned task done completely. Being insistent means making sure that you are obeyed completely!

Being Consistent

From the beginning of the awareness of their world, children regularly push against the rules, regulations, and confinements of that world. Parents are there to keep them safe, to teach them humane behavior, and to mold their character. As you learn to be consistent in your responses to situations that repeat themselves, you confirm to your children that their world is a safe place and you can be trusted. On the other hand, if one time you discipline and the next you are indifferent, you are revealing a hot/cold response to disciplining that children will take advantage of whenever possible: "But Mom, last time you . . ."

If you are consistent, children come to trust you. The first time you say, "John, we do not get into the pantry without permission. If you would like to get into the pantry for some crackers, please ask," you are setting a precedent for how you deal with John's response to hunger and his desire to get into the pantry.

The second time you say, "Remember, John, you can open the pantry door only after you have asked permission. You seem hungry. What should you ask me?" you are reinforcing the rules in your home that allow for order and consistency.

The third time you say, "John, you remembered to ask before you got a snack from the pantry. That makes me happy. You may have a second snack pack if you want!" you are confirming to him that he understands the appropriate responses to his hunger and the limitations of the kitchen pantry rules. He is safe, he understands the family rules, and he will likely continue to ask before getting into the pantry because you have affirmed that this is the sure way to your approval.

Parents also need to keep their promises to their children. If you indicate that tomorrow you are taking them to the movies as a treat, you will lose the trust of your children if tomorrow you suddenly attach going to the movie to their having completed all their chores in a timely manner. You are being inconsistent if the movie changes in one day from a gift to a measured, earned reward. If you had said initially that you were taking the family to a movie if everyone contributed to the cleaning of the house, with each member in charge of dusting, vacuuming, and cleaning up one room, then you can hold to that standard for going to a movie as a reward. Promises should be made carefully, held to fiercely, and rarely be changed at a later time to include the addition of more work. Is the movie free or do your children have to wonder if such a treat will be taken away if they don't clean up appropriately?

Children also benefit when routines in the home are followed in nearly the same pattern, with the same timing, day after day. This is especially true when children are very young. They settle into routines when dinnertime happens around 6 P.M. each evening, baths are next, and books are read in bed with friendly parental voices and hugs. This consistency should last even as children enter school and have extracurricular activities. Dinnertime might be later but should still include the whole family whenever possible. This ensures that children see the family as a cohesive whole at least once a day.

This consistency can extend to rituals of morning and evening kisses, hugs, and prayers. It might include talking together before they leave in the morning and when they return in the afternoon or evening. It might be any number of activities, but they should be special to your family and they should happen again and again.

Being consistent means making sure that you are obeyed every time! It means following through when you make promises so your children learn they can trust you. With this mutual trust, consistency in behavior becomes a pattern of your family life, and both parents and children know they mean what they say.

Being Persistent

A parent's job is difficult, long-term, and often frustrating. Children will try many ruses, in many different circumstances, to see just how persistent you are at repetitive discipline. If you react appropriately one time, can they expect that you will react again in the same way? Just one slip, just one time, will undo many times of regular parental responses.

When parents allow children to use vulgar language without doing anything about it the first time, or allow children to sneak a snack from the freezer without addressing the issue immediately, or feel that they can wait until the children get a little older to discipline them if they leave a messy bathroom "because there has been so much stress lately" . . . well, those parents are asking for trouble.

When you say, "Derek, that word is not permitted in our home," you are setting a firm foundation of verbal behavior. Derek, of course, is likely to say the word again, perhaps out of eyesight but within your hearing. If you are too distracted or weary to return to the situation and discipline again, you are teaching Derek that you will not be persistent in sustaining the standards you have set. A persistent parent would say,

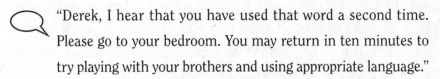

"Derek, I hear that you have used that word a second time. Please go to your bedroom. You may return in ten minutes to try playing with your brothers and using appropriate language."

This persistent parenting helps children to know that you are aware

of their inappropriate behaviors and are willing to shape their world for their betterment. And you will do it again and again until they comply.

If Derek returns to the group and shortly thereafter says the unsuitable word a third time, you must be firm.

> "Derek, I'm afraid you don't understand. That word is not permitted in our family. You will need to return to your bedroom again, this time for twenty minutes. Then you may come to me and ask to 'try again' before playing with your brothers."

With this persistence, you are affirming that, indeed, foul language will not be allowed in your home, now, later, or ever.

Occasionally letting children choose their consequences can help to reinforce the principles you are trying to teach. Of course, they might choose something too harsh or too easy, but you could settle on an appropriate consequence inbetween.

> "Staying in your room until Christmas won't work, Derek, and we know that staying in your room again for a few minutes hasn't worked either. We just tried that. How about if you picked up one hundred rocks in the backyard and brought them to me in this bucket? Then you may try again playing with your brothers and speaking properly when you are with them."

The discipline that you choose together is usually effective even when it is symbolic, because it reminds your children that discipline will happen again and again until they correct their behavior.

In addition, other siblings are watching, listening, and learning that their parents don't tolerate "that word" in the home and that they are likely to be picking up rocks, too, if they use certain words in their parents' hearing. The parents have proven themselves to be persistent when they see inappropriate behaviors repeated.

Both parents must mutually support each other in their

persistence. There is trouble when the mother says after the father has disciplined his son, "Oh, John, you are so hard on Derek. He really is tired after a long day of school and what is one bad word, anyway, when all his friends are saying far worse?" If you do disagree with what your partner in parenting is doing, those opinions should be expressed privately between the two of you later. A discussion can follow as to the standards your family will set and how you as parents see your roles in supporting each other in your parenting style. Perhaps more important than the methods you use in disciplining is the persistence you incorporate to help your children see that the rules have been made and will be enforced. These walls of safety, as I call them, give security to the children. Children are often frightened and saddened by events in their lives. Parents' persistence in making sure that rules are followed and that the standards are met offers a more secure environment no matter what other problems occur in your children's lives.

Being persistent means making sure that your standards are complied with over and over and over again!

As a result of these improvements in your parenting style, parents who are insistent ("Yes, you must pick up ALL your toys"), consistent ("Yes, we pick up the toys in the family room every evening just before Dad comes home"), and persistent ("No, you may not watch TV just this one time before cleaning up your toys") have the opportunity to more successfully nurture their family.

Be insistent. Make sure you are obeyed completely.

Be consistent. See that you are obeyed every time.

Be persistent. Continue to monitor your children until your standards are understood completely and are met again and again.

Be the parent your children need in order to find well-being and security under your influence.

CHAPTER SIXTEEN

Make the Unpleasurable More Pleasurable

Each child is truly unique, and your job as parents is to make that exclusive individuality shine as much as possible as your children grow and stretch themselves into new and interesting areas of development.

One of the most important gifts you give to your children is your own attitude about life's mundane and repetitive tasks. If you complain, they will learn to complain. If you are half-hearted and somewhat slovenly, they will learn that such habits are acceptable in their lives. If you raise your voice, object, and make smart-aleck comments, they will do likewise.

On the other hand, if you are cheerful and greet each new day as an adventure, they will see their own lives in such a manner. If you tackle problems and see them through to a workable solution, they will also figure out how to solve challenges. If you describe the satisfaction you feel with a household chore well done, they will find the same satisfaction in doing their personal chores well. If you personally reward yourself after finishing a particularly difficult chore, they will learn that *if* they do their work, *then* they can also anticipate doing something pleasurable afterward.

They are watching and learning first by your own example. Be mindful of your own routines and responses and lay a solid foundation by passing on your standards in personal grooming tasks, daily household responsibilities, and regular weekly chores. This helps your children soar to greater heights because the essentials of daily living are taught and practiced and will eventually become habitual in their lives. When individual responsibilities are completed, there is more order, more time, and more interest in creativity and accomplishment. Because the dishes are regularly done, the rooms are routinely cleaned, and homework is completed, there is more time left over for diversions of the nicest kind.

For example, it takes only a short time to make a bed once you have learned how, only minutes to bathe and dress for the day's needs, and only a bit longer to straighten up your personal environment before emerging to face the day. It is parents' opportunity to make "work" a natural, even enjoyable, part of every day and to help children feel good about their day-to-day accomplishments in keeping things orderly.

As a parent, you can also help tremendously by training your children in three principles: the joy of turning any job into a game, the excitement of doing it faster this time than last, and the pleasure of doing a bit extra to "finish with a flourish."

Make Any Work a Game

Children's imaginations are very active, especially during the first several years of their lives. You can take advantage of this by turning any and all work into a game. The kitchen floor that needs sweeping can become a ice hockey rink that needs to be "iced" right before the famous players begin their weekly practice. The front room table that needs dusting can be a ballroom dance floor being prepared for tiny fairy ballerinas just putting on their shoes. A bath can be a scuba diving event with applause for the deep sea swimmer who washes his own body, hangs up his towel after drying himself, and puts the floor mat over the edge of the tub without being prompted. ·

Remember, too, that "if" and "then" are great motivators. If there is something that must be done, attach it to something that will be more pleasurable afterward.

"Lindsay and Marianne, we must get these dishes done soon. If you can get them done in the fifteen minutes before your favorite TV show begins, then I don't mind if you watch it for a half hour while I finish up the mending."

It is so delightful to be in a family that is "playing" while at work. Of course, you might have to rustle up your somewhat rusty imagination to teach children how to play at their work. But, oh, the fun that children can have as they vacuum up "gold dust," find dirty "millipede" socks for the Mama Millipede, or set the table for "Papa Bear" who is sure to give them a tickle if dinner is "just right."

Help Things Along

So many times children struggle with starting their chores. They are not sure where to start, exactly what to do, or how to incorporate the best methods. This is where a parent's influence, example, and training are very important. With very young children, set up a specific schedule for the completion of today's jobs. For example, Lily may be too young to make her bed, and so her personal responsibilities could begin with getting up so Mom can make the bed while Lily is getting dressed.

> "Lily, we begin the day by getting out of our beds, taking off our pajamas, getting dressed, washing our faces, and combing our hair."

This repetitive practice provides security and stability to everyday routines. With practice, the chores take less and less time. Initially set the standards by showing children how to do each job from beginning to end. Then, as the children become more competent, you can begin to train them how to do their jobs even more expeditiously. For example, Matt is ready to learn how to make his bed because he has been dressing himself for many months and is now good at doing that.

> "Matt, making your bed will now be your responsibility because you have turned three years old. We begin by sitting right on top of your pillows and pulling up your quilt until it is even across the top of the bed right at your knees. Then we climb off the bed, puff up your pillow, and put it at the top of your bed. See how most of your bedroom looks neat when your bed is made right. Now, let's get dressed for the day."

Talking about the best order for completing personal chores also lets children feel comfortable that there is an end to the chore and that when they are finished they will receive your approval.

> "Lizzie [a four-year-old], it's time to get the day started. Remember, we start by doing four jobs in your bedroom. We make your bed, open your blinds, shut the closet door, and put your books on the shelf. Then we get dressed and have breakfast. I'm making poppy-seed muffins this morning. I know they are your favorite."

Stating the sequence doesn't mean this is the only way to straighten up a bedroom and start the day, but it does mean this is the way you are doing it with this child right now. Day after day, as you train your children, if you do the same routines in the same order, the children become accustomed to these routines, will welcome your compliments and praise, and can begin to move toward self-responsibility.

> "Lizzie, your bedspread is lying flat, the blinds are letting in the sun, the closet door is tightly shut, and I don't see a single toy or book on your floor. I feel so good when I walk into this neat room. And I notice that you are already almost dressed, too. Wow!"

These specific compliments on the progress of your children as they learn the ritual of "how to start the day" will reinforce the desired pattern of work. Over and over again, Lizzie knows that she is validated as a member of the family as she successfully completes her morning routine.

When and if Lizzie fails to complete the established routine, you need to repeat what the standards for her jobs are and prompt her to continue her work until it is completed.

> "Lizzie, I see the bedspread is straight and neat, I can see a tree through the open curtains, and the closet door is shut. Oops, three books on the floor are still waiting for the 'bedroom librarian' to get them back on the right shelf."

You don't want Lizzie to learn she can get away with less than full obedience. As you watch, encourage, and sometimes even help things along with your gentle compliments and reminders of undone chores, you are moving Lizzie toward a shorter amount of time that she needs each morning to finish these jobs.

Sometimes a timer adds a fun motivator to get chores started and helps children realize that work doesn't need to take a long time—it just needs to be gotten to and finished. You might call these "five-minute miracles." (Or change it to ten-minute miracles or twenty-minute miracles to fit the job at hand.)

> "Lizzie, you have done your morning chores every single day this week. It's time to find out how long it takes you to finish. What do you think? Five or six minutes? I'll set the timer and we'll see."

This defined amount of "finishing" time then becomes the starting point for children to beat when they lack motivation or are grumpy. Once they are comfortable with their routines, they might just need a jumpstart once in a while, so use a motivator to make chores fun to finish!

Finish with a Flourish

This simple phrase, "finish with a flourish," can be used when encouraging children to move past doing "just enough" to "doing something extra." Encourage your son who is mopping the kitchen floor to find flowers in the backyard for a vase you will place on the kitchen table. Prompt the daughter who is vacuuming the hallway to also sneak-vacuum the laundry room without telling anyone about this extra service and thus become a "pixie helper." Persuade the son who is sweeping the front porch to swipe the broom at the cobwebs dangling from the porch light while he is at it, just for fun.

Discussing with your children the difference between doing the bare minimum at their chores or doing their very best and maybe a bit extra helps children realize that you desire them to strive to be doing something past the norm. Children usually respond quite well to this request, especially when they are asked to decide what the "flourishes" will be with their assigned jobs and then are encouraged to come and tell you about it afterward.

Come Back and Tell Me

It is no surprise that children need lots of attention during their lives. But children also need lots of praise for what they do. Because you will often be distracted with other responsibilities and may not be aware that they have begun their work, have done it well, and have finished it nicely, it is useful to train them to return and report to you. This brings their work onto your radar screen, and without much trouble you can inspect, praise, and compliment their efforts. Occasionally you will also have to correct and ask for a redo job, but this interaction—this back and forth as the training process continues—is most successfully done when the children come and tell you they are finished. It is then that you can reward them! Sometimes it will be with a treat, sometimes you will validate them with a hug and kiss, and sometimes you just use a sincere compliment. But set up the routines of your family so that opportunities continually come to review what has been done and to praise each child's efforts for the benefit of your family.

Making chores some sort of a game, using different kinds of motivation to get them started and on their way, and urging children to do their jobs with pride, satisfaction, and with "a final flourish" will make working in your home fun, exciting, and a lot more appealing.

CHAPTER SEVENTEEN

Have Better School-Morning Routines

So much chaos can happen when school-morning routines are established for the first time or are re-established as school time approaches each year. But chaos is not inevitable. With some simple changes in habits, some additional tools, and a system in place for independent behavior on the part of your children, school mornings can calm down considerably and become an enjoyable, loving time of the day. The following are several ideas to consider as you think about improving your own situation. As always, the goal is to make mornings easier by helping your children become independent and self-sufficient. Teaching these specific skills will help harried parents get their children to school on time with smiles on their faces and with less confusion and stress.

Make It Easier to Get Dressed

Whenever possible, make it easier for your children to get dressed. If your children are young, make up clothing packets for each day of the week. The packets should include an entire outfit: top, bottom, socks, and possibly underwear. Pack all of the weekly outfits in a closet sweater holder by Monday morning. This is especially useful for chil-

dren who are tired in the morning or are balky about getting ready for school. They now have one less decision to make every morning because what they are to wear has already been decided. Their shoes should be stored in one of the lower sweater holders. In colder weather, their coat and winter accessories should also be in a bottom holder.

With older children, the same principle applies but with some flexibility. Instead of making up packets for the week, independent children can set out the evening before what they will wear the next day. Children not so mature can be helped by their parents. Again, the tension of choosing under the duress of limited time is eliminated and morning routines are relieved of stress.

Children should all have the same morning goals: get up, make their beds, take off their pajamas and put them away neatly, dress themselves in that day's clothes, and put on their shoes.

Teach Children to Be Independent in the Kitchen

The next goal is to make it easy for children to get their own breakfast and then clean up after themselves if your family doesn't eat this meal together. Choose several cold cereals and store them in clear plastic containers. This makes finding the right cold cereal easier for everyone, especially if the cold cereals are stored at a lower, easy-to-reach location. Parents should have a backup box of all cereals stored up high at all times to save tears and tantrums if a sibling uses up all the cornflakes and there are none left for a later eater.

Teach children to serve their own breakfast and clean up after themselves every morning, including getting their own cold cereal, putting their bowl in the sink or dishwasher (which means that the dishwasher must be emptied beforehand), wiping the table where they sat, and pushing in their chair. Milk should be put away and the cold cereal container returned to its proper place. Everyone should do a little bit to keep the kitchen orderly.

Keep School Items Collected in One Place

Confusion is reduced when all items going to school the next day have a "home." You could have a labeled plastic container for each child for his or her school needs. When an apple is needed for a science project, put it in that child's plastic container. Permission slips go here, too, as do backpacks, jackets, and books.

Parents and children should work together to put all necessary school items in the proper containers until the habit is well established. Then the children should continue on their own to put all school needs, including backpack, science project items, and school library books in their personal school containers. This makes it easier to have everything collected that will be needed to leave for school each morning.

Make It Easier to Handle School Papers

Of all the challenges of school, handling papers seems to be at the top of most parents' list. To solve this problem, have a labeled, stackable letter tray for each member of the family. One of the parents' trays is usually at the top. When children come home from school, they are to put any papers needing a parent's attention (graded homework, tests, and permission slips) in that parent's tray. The parent then files obsolete paperwork, discards unneeded paperwork, and returns current

paperwork to the children's trays for them to see and put in their backpacks before bedtime.

Because school mornings are a time of great confusion and frustration until routines settle down, look at all your school-morning decisions and move them to the night before whenever possible. Look at where confusion reigns and find ways to eliminate or reduce it. Find tools to make it easy to handle the many papers associated with school. Work diligently to make school-morning routines easier and smoother wherever possible.

CHAPTER EIGHTEEN

Do Homework the Right Way

Homework Standards

When your children begin school, you will need to establish some important daily habits for homework completion.

Set up a place, quiet and secluded (but within your ever-watchful supervision), where your children can do their homework.

For instance, have a quiet hour after school when the kitchen table is the "homework" table with the rules of no talking, no face making, and no silly noises. In other words, there is a serious attempt to keep children focused on their homework.

Or you might let older children retire to their bedrooms to complete this work. A personal desk in your children's bedrooms is very helpful for homework. With a small overhead bookshelf, personal office supplies, and a good lamp, homework time also becomes a time to be alone and to think, wonder, and dream (which sometimes isn't exactly the idea). If children are left in their rooms until their homework is finished and they can't do anything else until then, they will soon get to the task.

When the homework is complete, check its correctness, and then talk to your children about what has been done, right and wrong. After they make the necessary corrections, children can then be allowed to pursue other activities.

Have a regular time for homework. Some families let their children play with friends for an hour after school and then the family gathers back home for homework. This tends to get out the wiggles, refresh their minds, and make them more likely to settle down to do homework.

Other families find that it is better to feed their children a snack, pull out the books, and get the homework done before any friends are allowed into the house or the children are allowed to go out and play.

Motivating with "before this happens, this must happen" is an effective technique for seeking cooperation. Children need some motivation that will keep their energy up through the homework process. It is helpful to always remind them of something intriguing or interesting that will follow. "We will watch a short video when you are finished!" "There is a piece of chocolate cake at dinner for everyone who gets their homework done and corrected before Dad gets home!" "You may have John over when your homework is done!" Set a pattern of homework first and then pleasures afterward.

Some children need more supervision and encouragement than others. Some children will struggle with a skill long past the normal time for children to be competent at that skill. Patiently work each day with those children, helping them and motivating them with attention and encouragement. It may take longer to get the homework done than usual, but once children understand the concept, they will turn out to be more competent and skillful than anticipated. Children hit their strides at different ages, but keep encouraging them to be diligent and self-motivated until they feel confident.

Set a time, set a place, get creative with motivators, and be patient with all of your children. Soon homework routines will become a natural part of your children's days and they will understand that you mean business when you say it is "homework time." And they will be much better students because of your diligence.

Every day you help them get through their homework, check it, and then have them correct it is one day closer to their turning out to be mature, delightful, creative adults who will thank you frequently for being there during this critical time of their lives.

One Right Answer

While there are many opinions about how to initiate teaching with children, I have found several techniques that are very successful. When there is only one right answer, as with spelling words or multiplication facts, give the right answer upfront rather than have children guess at the answer, get it wrong, and then have to learn it right the second time around.

$$2 \times 2 = 4$$

Memorization

Many times during a child's educational experience, memorization will be needed. A parent can help this process along the way by teaching children how to memorize from an early age. It is easier to start with simple rhymes or simple songs and then advance to longer and more complex ditties. This process of focusing on memorization can take place while driving in the car, walking to school, and waiting at the doctor's office. It can be fun, but it will take the creative nurturing of an interested adult.

The adult who teaches children to say the alphabet backward for instance, is teaching a valuable skill that can be used for filing, searching in a dictionary for words, or for other needs. And this parent is also having a good time showing a child that memorization is a process: review, try it, review again, try it more, review again, and finally get it.

> "Briana, we have to sit in the doctor's office for about ten more minutes before the doctor will see us. I'm trying to learn the alphabet backward. Do you want to join me? Let's write it out so we can have a reference sheet while we learn. What do you think will be the first three letters in our backward alphabet?"

Parents with children who have difficulty memorizing might help them learn some mnemonic devices, which are simple ways to remember things such as the order of the planets, the colors of the spectrum, and the order of operations in math, to name a few. Children might even create their own "remembering" games.

There is a lot parents can do to create a rich, full, endearing, and creative atmosphere for their children. They can help by setting the standards for homework, finding a good, quiet place for children to study, and correcting homework so the children have the right answers when they return to school. Carefully monitoring and encouraging homework time each day, teaching them the "right" answers the first time, and nurturing the memorization process will greatly enhance your children's formal education and make it fun to be in your house.

"Z, Y, X . . . here we go on the backward alphabet!"

CHAPTER NINETEEN

Use Family Councils and a Family Mission Statement

It has been my experience that families who hold weekly councils together significantly improve their children's cooperation in doing jobs, supporting rules, and working together on family projects. A family council is a time when as many family members as possible gather together to discuss items of general interest and need. It can be used to help the family address common issues together, and it has the advantage of keeping the family unified and informed about family events, activities, and pressures.

Family councils are best utilized on a regular basis, preferably weekly. Some families have them on Sunday night, others on Monday night before or after family home evening.

Weekly Family Council

The weekly family council is for all the people who live in your home. Everyone gathers in a room with comfortable seating where conversation can flow easily. This is the time that you will be making assignments, asking for commitments, and holding your children responsible for remembering to do their chores, finish their homework, and help out with occasional extra jobs around the house and yard.

The parents bring a large wall calendar to family council to make notes as all family members bring up their own commitments. When family council is finished, this calendar can be posted in a place easily viewed by everyone. Near the kitchen table is a great place for reviewing during evening meals together.

The parents also bring enough blank to-do lists for each member of the family to have for the upcoming week. A sample to-do list is on page 155. (These to-do lists are available as a free download at www .houseoforder.com.) In addition, all members of the family bring to family council their to-do lists from the previous week.

Some families find it helpful, when they start holding family councils together, to keep everyone's to-do lists in a central location for easy reference. This also allows parents to follow up on children's written commitments. Some parents even find it useful to sign off to-do list commitments before allowing children to have free time, play with a friend, or watch TV.

During family council, children should fill out their to-do lists. As they accomplish the tasks during the week, they can cross the items off, and have their parents sign them. When they come to the next session of family council they can tell the whole family about their progress.

Eventually, the children might want to keep their to-do lists in their bedrooms or their pockets. The concept, however, is to make up a list, work from it during the week, and still have it in hand for the following family council so the children can come back and tell about it.

Name _____

Month _____

My To-Do List

Sun	Mon	Tues	Wed	Thurs	Fri	Sat

_____

_____

_____

_____

_____

_____

_____

_____

_____

_____

_____

_____

_____

_____

_____

_____

_____

My To-Do List

30 Sept.	① Oct.	2	③	4	⑤	⑥
Sun	Mon	Tues	Wed	Thurs	Fri	Sat

- Piano lessons on Wednesday after school
- Gather supplies for science project (due on the 15th)
- Make my bed every day this week
- Help rake leaves with Dad on Saturday
- Help Mom with dishes on Mon, Wed, and Fri

My favorite to-do lists are usually half sheets (8.5" x 5.5") and have seven squares at the top. Since this is similar to one week of a monthly calendar, family members can visualize what the week looks like. As family council proceeds, each family member fills in the dates for the seven days of the week in the squares at the top of the page. As they receive assignments, make commitments, and want to jot down reminders, they will first circle the date to remind them there is something to do "on Monday" and then write down specific notes on the lined portion of the to-do list.

Usually, the parents begin family council by detailing their own commitments during the upcoming week and showing the family how these have been written on the family calendar. At this point, new to-do lists are handed out to family members. Additional family work projects and family fun activities can be discussed and added to the family calendar and the personal to-do lists. Parents can also inform children of extended family responsibilities during the week, such as extended family functions they will be attending together and letters or e-mails that need to be written to older siblings, missionaries, or grandparents who live far away.

Then, starting with the oldest child (so that he or she can be the "model" for younger siblings) and making sure everyone has a chance to share, family members have the opportunity to talk about their progress on their previous week's to-do list, discuss what they were able to accomplish, what their new goals are, and how they fared on their commitments. They can then discuss their upcoming activities (which can be noted on the family calendar), and fill out their new to-do lists for the new week regarding homework, school projects, extracurricular activities, church obligations, and household chores.

Other family members may cheer any progress that is made, make suggestions about ways to improve, and applaud each others' activities and accomplishments. This is a very important part of a family's success as you help your children learn to work, make commitments, support each other, and keep to the family standards.

As children begin their contribution to the family council, they can talk about homework assignments and their due dates, upcoming tests, and any other school projects. For example, one child might have an English paper due on Tuesday, a math test on Thursday, and a football game on Friday evening. Parents should make notes on the family calendar or on their own to-do lists to limit or eliminate outside activities and TV or computer game privileges on those nights when the stress will be particularly high because of an upcoming test or outstanding school project.

The children can also discuss their extracurricular activities and commitments, including goals for Faith in God, Scouting, Duty to God, and Personal Progress. This is the time for children to discuss their commitments to bring brownies for a church activity or earn ten dollars for the soccer coach's appreciation dinner. When these items come to the attention of the parents ahead of time, they can make accommodations in their own schedules. Maybe it will be easier to purchase premade brownies or buy a brownie mix. Maybe the brownies will need to be baked two nights before they are needed. Maybe Dad will need to invite a child to weed in the backyard at the rate of five dollars per hour to earn the needed ten dollars.

Parents can also remind their children to make notes on their to-do lists as they mature and are responsible for chores that happen only occasionally. For example:

 "Isaac, remember how you have committed to take care of our weekly trash removal? Your to-do list is a great place to note that on Wednesday you are to wheel the garbage can out to the street. If you make a second note on Thursday to bring it back to the side of the garage after you get home from school, then that job will be done nicely. Thank you for being so grown-up about handling this new responsibility."

"Emma, Wednesday is your piano lesson. How about using your to-do list to make a note on Tuesday evening to put your books in the car so when I pick you up at school on Wednesday, they will already be in the car?"

The to-do list also allows teenagers to note the days they might be out of the home working at a part-time job: for example, Monday, Wednesday, and Friday from 5 to 10 P.M. Writing this down could also remind them about rides they have to arrange.

To add some organization to the wall calendar, encourage your older children to write their commitments in their own special color on the family calendar. This allows all family members to see who is going where and when, and why Mom won't be home one afternoon when they get back from school.

When family councils are held regularly, children tend to make good use of this time to tell parents about their own lives. A little discussion during the council saves much stress and tension during the rest of the week.

Discuss Family Concerns

After commitments are discussed, work assignments are made, and other family activities are detailed, it is time to discuss family concerns. Parents and children should be given a chance to express what is on their minds regarding family conflicts. Train your children that when they join this discussion it should include a proposed solution, not just a complaint. For example, John might be having trouble with his twin brother's messy habits in their bedroom.

"Mom and Dad, Jake and I worked out a deal. I always keep my side of the room clean but Jake's bed is never straight and he keeps junk on his desk. We talked about it. I am going to make his bed and clean up his messy desk every morning and he is going to take my turn doing dishes twice a week. We both like the idea and we want to try it for one week. Okay?"

At other times the issues are too "hot" for resolution right at the moment, so the parents might choose to continue conversations between themselves and then resolve the issues with individual family members privately. This allows parents to discuss the needs between themselves, find an answer they mutually agree upon, and then unitedly approach the individuals involved regarding possible answers or solutions.

The Compliment Circle

The end of family council or family home evening is an excellent time for parents to compliment each other and their children. All family members should also say something nice about their parents and siblings. For example, Dad might start the compliment circle.

"Honey, I really appreciated the lasagna you served last night. It hit the spot, and I liked the soft, melted cheesy topping.

"Jordan, I appreciate not having to worry about taking the garbage out to the street any more, especially with my change in commute time. Your help makes a big difference.

"Sierra, thanks for practicing the piano this week. I particularly like the new ragtime piece you are playing. It made my toes dance Friday morning when I heard it.

"Dylan, thanks for the big hug this morning. I especially appreciate it when you remember to push in your chair after dinner."

Mother then has her turn to compliment each family member, as do all of the other family members. This may be the only time during the week that nice comments are made about family members, but such encouragement holds a family together and unifies them. It helps them look for the good in each other, which counterbalances the times they have conflict.

There are other important activities that can strengthen family unity. Each of these projects helps children understand their place in the family circle and contributes to their self-esteem.

Family Mission Statement

It is very beneficial for every family to have a family mission statement. This helps you focus your family's values, goals, and ambitions in a particular direction. It identifies your focus and organizes your energy so that each member of the family can identify with something good and noble. It doesn't have to be long or complex.

Here are four points to organizing and preparing a family mission statement.

1. Consider basing your mission statement on either a scripture such as "But in our house, we will serve the Lord" (Joshua 24:15) or a noble statement such as "Return with Honor." This saying can be learned by even the youngest or most reluctant member of the family. It is the first step to clarifying a mission statement.

2. The mission statement could continue and state the positive characteristics you value in your family: honesty, integrity, a high work ethic, compassion, or whatever characteristics you want your family focus to be. Describe what values you would like them to be true to,

what standards you hold dear, and what you hope they will emulate as they mature.

3. The family mission statement might also describe some family goals, such as higher education, missions, and temple marriages.

4. The family mission statement might also describe some areas of family unity. Some examples are "in our family we are kind and considerate of each other," or "in our family we work together until the job is done right," or "in our family we respect each other's needs," or "in our family we don't hit." Use wording you feel would work for your family to identify your family as special and unique and bring them closer to your and your spouse's long-term desires for your children.

Think about the long-lasting value of a family mission statement. Speak to your spouse about it, inquire of your children, and then use some of the pointers mentioned here to make your own statement.

Family Symbols

In addition to a family mission statement, many families also benefit from having a family flag (with colors and symbols representing family values), a family song, and even a family motto. This desire to unify your family on an ongoing basis and to clarify the specific family activities that encourage such unity will help a great deal as you raise the children with the qualities you desire them to have.

PART FIVE: *Teach Them*

CHAPTER TWENTY

Teach Them to Live Simply

I cannot overemphasize the need for children to have a simple world. They need to be able to readily identify those who love them, where they live, what they own, who corrects them, and how much is expected of them. As you help your children discover their world, it is especially important to keep three specific areas of children's lives simple: clothing, possessions, and routines and rituals. This will help them feel both serene and safe.

Clothing

Children's lives will be simpler when they have fewer items of personal clothing to worry about. When they are very young, their comprehension of numbers doesn't often extend beyond their age. For this reason, limit the number of items in their personal clothing drawer. Three-year-old preschoolers can easily handle three pairs of pants, three tops, three pairs of socks, one pair of shoes, and three pairs of underwear. You will probably have more of their clothing stashed away, but in their small world, they will need only a few options. A single sweater, a coat for outdoors, and some dressier clothing for church and nice occasions will be enough.

Try to have all of the tops and bottoms match each other so that no redressing is necessary for your children to look coordinated when they begin to dress themselves. When children's wardrobes are simple, it is possible to quickly and easily teach them to fold and stack their tops in a drawer, place the folded pants beside them, and put their socks in the little box you have provided for them in the drawer. Their underwear can likewise be folded and stacked. You might need to teach them several times to fold their clothes when they are freshly washed and dried, to put them in their drawer, and to shut the drawers so that they learn that all clothing returns to a place of order after being cleaned.

As your children mature and begin their formal education, the number of clothing items might be increased to match their new status, usually five outfits during the elementary school years. This could be increased to ten outfits when children enter junior high and even more when they enter high school, if circumstances allow.

But, as much as possible, keep children's clothing life simple. They don't need multiple pairs of shoes. They usually have trouble keeping track of one pair. They don't need multiple coats; fewer coats mean that they will come to appreciate and care for their coat because it is their only one.

Possessions

Simplify your children's life by limiting the number of their possessions. Help your children form attachments, not gather collections. This is essential because children don't feel as much responsibility for their possessions when they have too many multiples of the same item. They don't take special care of their toys because breaking one won't impact their capacity to play since a dozen others of the same kind are laying around within reach. Especially for children, less is more.

A single, threadbare teddy bear with only one eye will be more beloved by a young child than a collection of stuffed animals, because children grow less and less able to attach as the number of possessions grow. They will still understand the concept of ownership and be very defensive of their possessions, but often they become simply owners and lose the sense of affection that is so essential to establishing meaningful relationships with others.

It becomes especially difficult to keep children's lives simple when generous relatives continue to inundate your children with more and "better" toys. As a parent, it is up to you to control, monitor, and contain this situation. Sometimes the excess toys can be stored; sometimes they can be sent "on vacation" and brought out again at a later time. Sometimes current toys can be put away to make room for the latest gizmo. But within your children's realm, the toys should be just enough and not too many.

Routines and Rituals

A lot can be said about the value of having routines and rituals in children's lives. From cutting peanut butter and jelly sandwiches the "right" way, to the proper procedures for bathing, getting on pajamas, and reading bedtime stores, simple routines and rituals bring a sense of security and safety into children's lives.

Each set of parents will decide what their routines and rituals will be, and occasionally these will change as circumstances do. One family struggled when the mother began working in the evening while the father worked during the day. Their only son, who was eighteen months old at the time, didn't understand why it was now Dad who got him into his pajamas, read him a story, and then tucked him into bed, when in the past his mother had performed such duties and shared tender moments with this child. The confusion was obvious in the child's initial refusal to accept his dad's attentions and in his occasional outbursts from time to time asking, "Where's Mommy?" He just missed his mom during bedtime. With continued patience and some prompting from Mom about their previous bedtime routines and rituals, the father was able to help the child adjust to the new situation by replicating her rituals until the child was more comfortable and confident with his father's unique routines.

In much the same way, you can settle the anxious feelings of your children, especially during stressful times, by continuing to follow the routines and rituals that have always been a part of your family's lifestyle.

Whether it is praying together in the morning before Dad leaves for work or reading a good book together during afternoon snack time after school, whether it is Dad's famous pancakes on Saturday morning or Mom's buttered popcorn on Sunday evenings, be sure to provide simple and repetitive routines and rituals for children to depend on. It is one of the ways you can keep life stable for them and how they learn to trust that you will be there for them day after day.

Make It Simpler for Everyone

As you make decisions about your children's clothing and possessions and establish routines and rituals, keep an eye out for other ways to simplify family life. The following are some easy, creative ideas that have made a tremendous difference in some very busy homes.

Identifying Color. Consider having an identifying color for each family member. Let each child choose his or her favorite color. For example, Dad's color might be green, Mom's pink, Olivia's yellow, and Alex's blue. When it is time for toothbrush purchasing, these colors are the favored ones. Then when a green toothbrush is left out on the bathroom counter, everyone in the family knows that Dad left his toothbrush laying around. When the toothbrush is yellow, Olivia is the culprit.

Water Cups. Have specific places for the water cups of each family member both near the kitchen sink and in the bathroom most frequented by that family member. This will save on dishwashing and encourage individual responsibility in both of these rooms.

Car Seating. Consider having one designated seat for everyone in the car, with a weekly rotation to reduce or eliminate arguments about "It's my turn." For example, James sits in the front seat on Monday and Wednesday, Hannah has it Tuesday and Thursday, and Mike gets Friday, Saturday and Sunday (unless both parents are in the car, in which case Mike relinquishes the front seat to a parent).

Dinnertime. You might want to specify a seating arrangement at the kitchen table that is rotated once a month. For example, one smart mother labeled napkin holders with the names of her family members so the child who set the table could place them where everyone sat before they all congregated at the table. This helped alleviate comments such as, "No, it's my turn to sit here" while the mother finished final dinner preparations.

TV Watching. You might have designated spots for everyone to sit in the family room while watching videos and movies. These could be changed on a rotating basis, but the decision about who sits where is made before the event, not fought about while everyone is trying to get settled.

Keep a watchful eye for these and other useful ways to make your family's life simple, because simpler is always better.

CHAPTER TWENTY-ONE

Teach Them to Wait Longer

An essential skill for children, teenagers, and even most adults is the skill of patiently waiting. One of the great challenges of parenthood is knowing when and how you can teach those you love to wait, especially if they are calling for you, demanding from you, or requiring your immediate attention. Let's divide waiting into three kinds: short-term waiting (usually just minutes), medium-length waiting (usually an hour or so), and long-term waiting (which might be from one day to one month).

Short-term Waiting

You start teaching this waiting skill by having very young children wait, if only momentarily, before you meet their demands. You might talk to Connor as you are preparing his bottle, reassuring him that the bottle is coming, but it will be one more minute before the water will be warm, the lid screwed on appropriately, and the mixture shaken enough. In your patter with your child, you might say,

"Connor, I'm fixing your bottle right now. You are being such a good boy and waiting so patiently, and I know it's hard. Soon the bottle will be ready, and you won't have to wait any longer."

As you interact with children day to day, look for opportunities to teach this very important principle. For instance, you might hold them off from eating the afternoon snack for a few minutes until the appointed time.

"Kayla, it's almost time for a snack with your sister. It will be a few more minutes before we will eat. How about if we wipe off your little table and put some fun napkins down? Let's get out the juices and cheese first and then call Emma to join us for a snack."

As children become more capable of understanding the concept of waiting, you might say,

"Chase, I would be happy to come and help you mold more clay. However, I have about three more minutes of folding towels, and then it will take me about two more minutes to put them away, and then I'll be there to see your clay shark."

This teaching about "waiting" allows you to reach a finishing point yourself so you can more effectively pay attention to your children. You have also helped them understand that waiting is a part of life.

Medium-length Waiting

It is vital for children, especially as they begin school, to learn to wait until the next day for some anticipated item, activity, or special occasion. After all, holidays and birthdays come only once a year, and to young children that seems like forever. Learning to wait, even until tomorrow, will settle patterns in their minds of how to work through anticipation and desire, even when the event will not happen until the next day.

> "Trevor, I won't be going grocery shopping until later today. I know that you like having Cheerios for breakfast, but they are all gone. There are Rice Krispies or toast for today's breakfast. Which one would you prefer? No, I'm not going to the store just to buy some more Cheerios. I'm sorry that all the Cheerios are gone, but we will have them again tomorrow morning for breakfast. Do you want toast or Rice Krispies today?"

Long-term Waiting

Children who regularly receive the "please wait" answer from their parents can learn to be satisfied, at least partially, with the reality of their situation. This capacity to delay gratification, taught by the parent and later self-initiated, helps children gain personal discipline. Parents should help children understand why it is important for them to save up their money before buying desired treasures, finish their homework before going outside to play, or complete their chores before watching TV.

> "Taylor, I'm so glad that you have finished your homework early, but we will not be watching TV until tomorrow night. Then we will watch a movie together as a family. Remember, we talked on Sunday about keeping the TV off on school nights this week so that Ben and Reece can finish their science projects. Since the TV is distracting when it is on, you committed to read or do something else when your homework was finished."

In regard to spending money, parents should not to indulge their children immediately in their desires, but help them learn to wait.

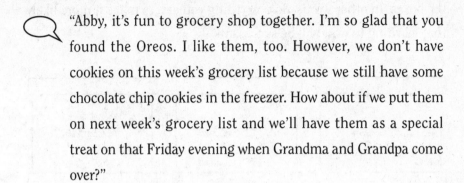

"Abby, it's fun to grocery shop together. I'm so glad that you found the Oreos. I like them, too. However, we don't have cookies on this week's grocery list because we still have some chocolate chip cookies in the freezer. How about if we put them on next week's grocery list and we'll have them as a special treat on that Friday evening when Grandma and Grandpa come over?"

Waiting by Design

Storing away half of your children's toys teaches the principle in a different way. If your children are cooperative, let them decide which of their toys are "going on vacation." Pack them away where they are out of sight. Tell your children that those toys will come back out to play later, maybe at a "Christmas in July" celebration. If your children don't understand, privately store away half of their toys for a period of time. This procedure allows for more creativity, with less mess, thus saving hassle for parent and children during cleanup.

Another way to approach "waiting" is to divide the playroom toys into several boxes, giving each box a label such as Baltimore, Philadelphia, Yucatan, Mississippi, England, New Hampshire, and Mozambique. The toys are divided into these boxes and all of them put away but one. This box is left out for your children to play with, and as soon as the toys in this box are picked up and put away, another box may be brought out and enjoyed. This eliminates a great deal of the mess in the house, keeps play time more lively and focused, and also teaches children to "clean up" as easily as they "mess up." Besides, the children are learning to pronounce long and difficult words with ease and can also learn a bit of geography as they read and say the names on the boxes. In other words, do everything you can to make it more likely that learning to wait will be successful!

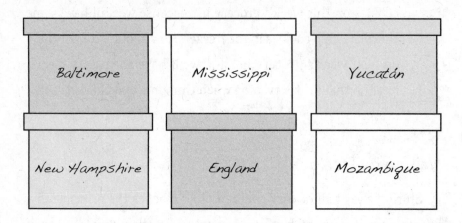

Respect for Mutual Waiting

As you teach this waiting skill, you will find that your children will begin to ask you to wait, too. You teach your children to respect you when you ask them to wait, even as you respect them when they ask for some time: "Mom, I'm just about finished with this chapter in my book. Can I take my shower in about five minutes?"

When you reply positively and then hear the bath water run in about five minutes you know you have accomplished two goals. Your child has understood and is responding to the "waiting" principle and has also become disciplined enough to keep promises. Such small but simple interactions, filled with mutual trust, go a long way to help children understand, comprehend, and accept that some of life is spent in waiting.

CHAPTER TWENTY-TWO

Teach Them to Share Better

Sharing is not natural for most young children, but there is a way to help this principle become more a part of their characters. Simple, repetitive experiences in sharing will go a long way to move children to understand the tremendous importance of patience, splitting treasures down the middle for other people's enjoyment, and giving up what they own to another.

You can introduce this skill by helping young children desire to share temporarily, to share by dividing, and then to share by giving away. Since most children don't learn the skill of sharing until they feel a sense of ownership, real sharing can only follow real ownership. So first you help your children understand that their birthday gifts do belong to them. They are theirs to use as they desire, and they may choose not to share right away. It is important that they have a period of feeling in control of their possessions before they can truly share them.

At the same time, to teach the skill of sharing, you can also casually converse using sharing examples from your own life. If Jared refuses to share his new toys with his brothers, you might say,

"Wow, I sure appreciate it when someone shares with me. Last night Dad gave me half of the last piece of cake. Yesterday, Tom let Jason hold his special truck for a minute, and Friday Elizabeth gave away two books she had finished reading."

Then, to continue to impress the need for this skill in the lives of your children, you can generously share with them.

"Jared, there is only one peach left and I know that you really like fresh peaches. I would be happy to split it with you. Here, take this bigger half."

Over and over again, you model sharing. You share with your spouse, with your peers, and with your children. You also talk about sharing whenever possible. It is only then that you can begin to impress upon your children the need for sharing.

Beginning Sharing Skills

When teaching the variables of sharing, first teach children how to share when there will be no personal loss.

For example, two children might each be given six crackers in a clear zipper-lock bag, but each child has a different type of cracker. If they each share three crackers with their companion, they will still have six crackers, three of each kind.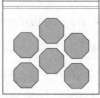

After children feel comfortable with sharing when there will be differences but not loss, then give them the chance to share when there will be no personal loss, but the results will not be even.

For example, two children might each be given five crackers, with each child having a different kind of cracker. Now the children will still have five crackers when they share, but they will have two of one kind of cracker and three of the other kind.

Finally, give children the chance to share when they will experience some personal loss. This is an interesting situation and often one that will need to be repeated over and over again, sometimes with the children on the "gain" end of division, and sometimes on the "loss" end of division.

For example, one child might be given six crackers and the second child be given five crackers. Now when they attempt to share, the six-cracker child can divide evenly but the five-cracker child will have to decide whether to give up three and keep two or keep three while she gives up two.

Initially, offer the opportunity to the five-cracker child to share more abundantly with the second child with words such as,

> "Brooklyn, it's Jody's birthday today. How about letting her have the extra cracker from your bag?"

Brooklyn may or may not share in this way, but you have suggested a possible opportunity for sharing.

Creative children might take the extra cracker and divide it in half, thus solving the problem of uneven opportunity. If they do, applaud their creativity as they share. If they keep the majority of the crackers and share the minority of the crackers, don't despair, there will be plenty of chances for future sharing experiences, especially if you continually provide such opportunities day to day. If the children prove to be generous, you might say,

> "Brooklyn, you were so generous today with your crackers, I think I will give you an extra portion of dessert tonight. Wow, I was just so impressed when I saw you share in this way."

If they don't feel and act as generously as you would like, you could proffer,

> "Brooklyn, sometimes sharing your extras is hard. Maybe another day you will feel more like giving up the extra cracker. And sometimes Jody will feel like giving up her extra cracker too."

Sharing Temporarily

Young children learn to share their toys, the sandpile, the bath, and their food with others by instruction and repetition. When there is only one toy and two eager children, the initial "your turn" and "his turn" principle of temporary sharing can be taught.

> "Tyler, there is only one red truck. I can see that both you and Sam want to play with it now, and Sam has it in his hand. Here is a blue truck for you to play with now. I'll set the timer for five minutes and then we will trade. You will get the red truck and Sam will get the blue one for the next five minutes. Fair enough?"

Sharing by Division

Children also need to learn the sharing principle of division. For instance, when food is served, dividing it in two to accommodate both children offers another chance for children to learn to share. Dividing the cookie in half is how the dilemma of two children and one cookie is solved. Parents would do well to talk this through as the cookie is divided and shared.

> "Paul, there is only one cookie left for the two of you. If you want, I will let you break it in half, and then we will let Shaun decide which half he wants for himself. Next time we have dessert we will let him divide it in half and you may decide which half you would like."

Sharing by Giving Away

Another type of sharing is the complete giving up of items that are dearly loved. When you encourage children to let go of some of their excess for the benefit of another child or a worthy purpose you are teaching them the deepest joy of sharing. (Initially, they may have some trouble recognizing and appreciating the joy that comes with that kind of sharing.)

There are two natural times to do this, the weekend of Thanksgiving (in preparation for the upcoming holidays) and the week before their birthdays (when they will be more likely to share willingly). Other opportunities will come now and again and should be used to help family members contribute their unneeded possessions to others.

It is also useful for children to see the actual recipients of their gifts. A drive to the poorer part of town, a walk down the hallway of a children's cancer hospital ward, or an article about a neighborhood house fire pinned to the refrigerator all offer opportunities for children to feel compassion and a desire to share.

Most children can gain more generous natures when these kinds of opportunities to give personal items away are proffered. Let them keep their bare, one-eyed teddy bear, but encourage them to donate several other stuffed animals that don't see much use or get much of their affection. One treasured truck will be worth more to your child, especially when he delivers to another child the fleet of other cars that have long sat idle in his closet.

Children will learn to share best if taught by your example. In other words, you need to give up what *you* love and cherish, when circumstances present such an opportunity, so that your children can see how and what to do. Whether it is sharing temporarily, sharing by division, or sharing by giving up treasures completely, learning to share molds a child who can love by giving generously.

Sharing through Rejoicing Together

A final way to share is to involve all family members in a child's personal accomplishment, even while rewarding the child. A child may talk about his personal achievements as he hands out a treat to everyone else before giving himself that same treat.

A wise mother, when giving a treat to her toilet-training younger child, would encourage this sharing by saying,

"Gavin, you are such a big boy for using the toilet and I am going to give you a treat, right after you wash your hands. In fact, let's share a treat with everyone in the family, and you can tell them about what you did just now.

"After you have told everyone about what you did and you have given them a treat, you can have the last two pieces of candy, one for sharing and one for using the potty."

CHAPTER TWENTY-THREE

Teach Them to Save More

Children who learn to be fiscally responsible from the time they are very young will have excellent habits formed by the time they are grown. A great way to start is to help all children realize that money given to them for a specific occasion, say a birthday gift, can be spent freely after ten percent is set aside to pay tithing. However, when children begin to regularly receive allowance or earn small amounts of money around the home, it is time to help them understand simple but important budgeting concepts. With younger children, one of the best ways to accomplish this is to prepare three labeled jars for dividing money when it is earned or received as an allowance.

Sharing and Saving

When you give money to young children, it is best to give it to them in change so that they can divide it into three amounts to be put in three separate containers. For instance, if Matthew earns one dollar, give him ten dimes so he can learn basic budgeting principles.

Decide together how much should be set aside for sharing, how much should be put away for savings, and how much is theirs for spending. A common division is to put 10 percent in tithing and 30 percent in savings, and keep 60 percent for spending. That means one dime will go in the first jar, three dimes in the second, and six dimes in the last jar. This leaves enough for immediate gratification and yet allows for charitable and saving habits to be established.

Using simple, prepared containers will help young children realize that all their money is not for immediate use. They need to save some for later needs, and some should be set aside for sharing. The two concepts of tithing and savings are essential to instilling fiscal responsibility into the characters of children.

If a more ample allowance is given to children with the understanding that they pay for some of their needs, a fourth container (for their personal expenses) might be included. Then they might divide their earnings as follows: 10 percent for tithing, 30 percent for savings, 30 percent for personal expenses, and 30 percent for spending.

It is useful to help even young children keep simple written records. Give children a small notebook so that you can help them record what they earn and what they do with their money. This will also give children practice in adding and subtracting and figuring percentages.

"Sarah, you worked hard for the five dollars Grandma paid you for raking her lawn. Let's turn the five dollars into quarters so you can divide them for your money jars. Then let's make a note in your money book. It looks like you will have three dollars for spending after you put fifty cents in your tithing jar and one dollar and fifty cents in your savings jar. If you decide to spend your three dollars when we go to the store, we'll write that in your notebook too."

Sarah's Money

Date	Item	Income	Expenses	Balance
	Beginning Balance			$0.00
May 20	Rake yard	$5.00		$5.00
May 20	Tithing		$0.50	$4.50
May 20	Savings		$1.50	$3.00
May 31	Spending (toy)		$3.00	$0.00

As children begin to have more income (usually in their early teenage years), either from paid jobs at home, babysitting, lawn mowing, or taking care of neighbors' animals or homes while they are on vacation, other containers can be added. At this point, teenagers should begin to take some responsibility for their own future education and vehicle needs. Children who save and contribute for some of their own

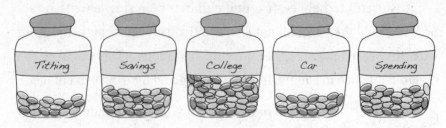

education and for some of their own transportation needs tend to appreciate those things more. In addition to saving for their own vehicle, if they borrow a family car they should also contribute some to gas, repairs, insurance, or tire replacement for the privilege of using a family vehicle. It is also a good idea for your children to move their coins occasionally from the savings jar into a savings account from an early age. Even young children can be taught the principle of accruing interest in an account. Then, as your teenagers move toward adulthood and become eligible for credit or debit cards, you will need to teach them about checks, debit cards, certificates of deposit, other investments, and how to handle debt effectively. You may even encourage them to use a computer spreadsheet to handle their increasingly complex budget. Categories might include:

- Tithing (and other charity or community contributions)

- Short-term savings (for example, personal computer needs)

- Mission

- Long-term savings (larger purchases, unknowns)

- College (technical school or higher education)

- Vehicle (fuel, maintenance, or purchase)

- Marriage (rings, honeymoon, household start-up costs)

- Spend (keep as cash)

Save before You Spend

The teenage years are the time to teach how to put money away in the bank, usually in several different accounts, before spending. It is time to teach the principles of preparing and keeping a more complex budget on the computer or on paper. It is time to teach how to balance the checking and savings accounts on a regular basis. Discuss with your children what percentage of earned money will go into each account. A good ratio might be:

- 10% tithing

- 10% short-term savings

- 10% mission

- 10% long-term savings

- 20% college

- 20% vehicle

- 10% marriage

- 10% spending

While each family will have different financial goals and different methods for teaching fiscal responsibility, the teaching must begin very early and the habits instilled for keeping records, saving, and sharing. Discussions should center around immediate, intermediate, and future needs. Children who are raised with these principles in their backgrounds and who handle their money with the careful supervision and teachings of their parents will have a great foundation for financial success and constancy in their adult lives.

Invest Wisely in Products

If parents study and shop carefully before investing in a product, children will see a good example of the importance of spending carefully. When parents talk about how tools or products last a long time if properly maintained, and how they make life easier for the whole family, children can see the wisdom of carefully thinking through their own purchases.

Repair More, Replace Less

Additional principles of fiscal responsibility are taught in the home as parents encourage creative responses to items that break, are torn, or begin to fall apart. If the first response is always to replace the item, then children lose the opportunity to learn to mend, replace a broken fuse, or use duct tape to keep an item together and therefore functioning longer. Whenever possible, teach children to make a treasure or a tool last longer by repairing it instead of just discarding and replacing it.

"Zach, I see that there is a small hole in your pajamas. I'll teach you how to mend it so your pajamas will last a little longer. If you fix it now, the hole won't get any bigger and you might make them last until you get a new pair for Christmas. Every little bit helps right now. Here, this is how you thread a needle."

"Megan, the hem of your jacket is hanging down. Let's fix it so you can wear it to school on Monday."

Parents can significantly impact their children's fiscal success as adults by careful, consistent training as money comes into their children's hands.

CHAPTER TWENTY-FOUR

Teach Them to Cooperate Kindly

Kindness is a skill that should be nurtured whenever possible, beginning with the way you respect the needs of your individual children. This training begins the first time your children reach out and hurt someone else. It starts when they want to pick up an animal and are taught how to do so with gentleness. It begins when they are asked to wait so their grandmother can get into the car first and when they are shown how to hold doors open for others. It is as simple as that. Talk to them about the many kindnesses they can perform as you demonstrate kindness yourself. Your children should hear over and over again from you the elements of treating others kindly.

Naturally, you will be demonstrating kindness and gentleness in your relations with your spouse, other children, your peers, and extended family. But, you will also need to help your children see the advantages of being tender. When they pick up their first cat by the ears, you might say,

"Gently now. Put your hands under the cat's belly to pick it up and stroke the kitten from head to tail. Be gentle and you'll hear the cat purr."

When a child wants to hug and kiss the new baby, the same principles are employed.

"Emily likes you to touch her softly. Here, just a little touch will do."

Over and over again children should learn from their parents how to treat others.

Children who see their father open the door for their mother, watch their mother use "please" and "thank you" in all her interactions, and then are taught to do the same thing, will have a pattern of gentle kindness in their own routines. I observed one mother who was particularly sensitive to help her children use words of politeness in all their interactions. Over and over again she gently said to her young daughter,

"Remember, begin by saying please. When you are finished, remember to say thank you."

If they forgot temporarily, she was there to remind, cajole, and encourage. It was just part of the day-to-day, hour-to-hour interactions in their lives.

Consistently teaching kind behaviors will help children learn to respond almost automatically in this way as they mature. They will open doors for others, ask with a "please," and end with a "thank you." They will be kind by nature because they observed it in their parents' behavior and also were taught over and over again how to be kind themselves.

CHAPTER TWENTY-FIVE

Teach Them to Work Harder

As children mature and approach their teens, they have a greater need to be independent, self-assured, and competent. As a parent, you want this to happen too. So even as you teach them during the early years to be obedient, to do their jobs completely, to finish with a flair, and to become self-initiating, it is important to also introduce the element of being the best, hardest, and most diligent worker they can be in any situation they will encounter. More than any other skill, the ability to work hard, to work long, and to work past what is required will make them stand out in school, when they find summer jobs, and as they interact with other teenagers and adults. It will propel them into opportunities as nothing else can.

The capacity to have a good work ethic, especially in public situations, is first taught by observing this characteristic in parents. If you want your maturing children to know how to work hard at a "real" job, you must invite them to work with you as you complete projects together so they see how it is done.

Show and Tell

Parents must allow their maturing children to observe how to do more challenging, complex jobs first before they can fully comprehend how to do it themselves. Parents should explain what different jobs entail, show the teenagers how to complete the job, and then let them acquire the necessary skills by practice.

It is easy to let children stay in the world of simple, uncomplicated work, but there are car jacks, table saws, bread mixers, and electric knives to use. Make sure that your children understand the safety requirements for such complicated work, and then monitor them until you are comfortable with their skill level before you let them try something complex themselves. Because it is your job to work yourself out of a job as your youth mature, it will be useful to help your teenagers become competent in all sorts of work, including changing the oil in the car, mowing the lawn, handling money, and working longer hours than might be comfortable.

Working Together One on One

It is useful to teach the skill of working hard one on one because there will be opportunity to converse, discuss, and teach. Most children find great leverage in not working well when there is an audience of other siblings. Children who balk at work, whine about chores, and find other ways to sabotage any attempts on your part to teach them about work might need individual attention.

Most children are not bad; they just need more attention than they usually receive. It is your responsibility to give them attention while you teach them the value of working diligently now and when others employ them.

For example, you might say,

"Michael, I'm going to drive over to the store and pick up forty two-by-fours for framing the bedroom we are finishing. Then I'll be stopping at Mac's for an ice cream cone. Want to come have some fun with me?"

Your attitude that work is pleasurable will help your son want to come. The chance to be alone with Dad adds additional pleasure, and ice cream on a hot afternoon balances the anticipated work. In addition, Michael will be learning about how to choose straight wood, how to move aside less useful pieces of wood in a neat pile, and how Dad greets the store manager. He will hear comments from Dad about how useful Jake, an older teenager who works at the store, seems to be to the manager.

"Hey, Michael, did you see how fast Jake ran to the front of the store when they called for an extra cashier?"

Of course, Michael should also have his own pair of work gloves, so that could be a purchase made at the store before the wood is selected and purchased. But working with his father on a real project, hearing the attitudes of his father about completing a project to improve the house, and seeing other teenagers in an employment situation will be useful for Michael. It might even be good to say to the store manager in Michael's presence,

"Joe, this is my son, Michael. He's fourteen now and we're working together on finishing a basement bedroom. He might be applying for summer work in a couple of years, so keep an eye out for him. He's a hard worker."

Teach Them to Work in a Threesome

After your children are comfortable working one on one with you, it is time to begin working in threes. This new dynamic adds complication to any working situation and allows the parent to monitor, calm, and teach principles of decision-making, compromise, and generosity.

For example, a mother might say to her young daughter,

"Natalie, I've noticed that washing the dishes goes twice as fast when three are working together, and it is fun besides. It is your and Anna's turn to do dishes on Tuesday and Thursday. How about if we work together on both days and look for ways to make it easier and faster?"

This attitude of cooperation and willingness to look at possible ways to make work more efficient will help children want to accommodate their parent's desire for a cooperative effort. It also affords time to show how to work through issues such as a broken dish, a pan that didn't get properly scrubbed, and the small details of finishing up dinner that might otherwise be left undone. Initially, let Natalie and Anna decide which of the jobs they will each do as you clean up together and how they would like you to help. With you involved, these skills of working in a larger group can be successfully learned.

Teach Them How to Work toward a Group Goal

Children who can work in a larger group have gained a very important social skill. As you share with them the many aspects of a larger project (preparing the backyard for planting of lawn, for example), you are helping them see that all long, hard jobs are just a lot of smaller, shorter jobs.

In a family council, you might describe that week's projects in preparation for the backyard improvement. Remember, individual responsibility leads to group success, so different opportunities for work could be laid out and then the family members can choose what they would like to do.

"This week the weather will be cooler in the evenings. It looks like we will all be home on Wednesday evening and Saturday morning. Let's divide the backyard into six sections, one section for each of us. Let's draw straws to see which section will be each person's responsibility. Here is what needs to be done in each section: the rocks all need to be picked up, the weeds have to be hoed and raked up, and the ground smoothed a bit. I will be happy to train you on Wednesday evening and help you if you need it. When your section is done, I'll check it, and then you are free to return to other projects.

"Mom says she will help the three youngest with their sections. On Saturday, you can work on your section anytime it seems best for you. Just let Mom or me know when you are finished so we can inspect your work.

"If it all gets done by Saturday evening, I'll get the ingredients for root beer floats for everyone!"

Involve Them in the Preparation and Planning of Big Projects

As children mature, they often feel a desire to lead in work projects. This is a useful skill because the person at the top often has more challenges than anticipated. Let them lead whenever possible so they know how to do it well.

"Andrew, you are thirteen, and I can't believe how many years you have helped plant the vegetable garden. It will be time to plant the garden again in about three weeks. Would you like to sit down and make up a plan for which plants to put in this year, how to divide it up for weeding, and a schedule for watering? Let me know when you would like to buy the seeds and starter plants, and I'll drive you to the store."

Andrew will probably enjoy this new position of authority and will thrive on your trust that he has worked well enough by your side during the past few years that he is ready to take charge. In turn, this will transfer some of the burden of yard work from you so you can focus on other things, always keeping an eye on what Andrew is doing to keep the garden growing well.

Learning to work hard will serve your children well when they leave home for college, missions, or marriage.

CHAPTER TWENTY-SIX

Teach Them to Feel Grateful

Teaching children contentment and gratitude is a difficult and ongoing challenge in any home. However, several techniques will definitely make it easier for the children to learn this skill and will also lighten your load.

Tell Them Yes to Less

Do not be afraid of having to tell your children "no." This is important because most of their life will have "nos" in it. This also reinforces the principles of "wait," "not now," "maybe later," and "who knows when."

As a parent you might get into a "yes, but . . ." mode with your children. You say, "No." They counter with a "Yes, but this time it is an exception." You counter, they counter a second time, and soon you have lost the battle and the war. When you decide to say no and have said it, keep to your "no." If you are going to end up negotiating, then negotiate before you give your final pronouncement, not after.

"McKenzie, you may not go to the movies tonight. You have not finished your homework, you did not clean up your room last night, and you have not kept your commitment to practice the piano today. The answer is no."

Of course, the child will usually have excuses and explanations. Despite your need to gratify your children's needs, if you have already told McKenzie that movies are for those who keep their commitments, keep to your "no." She will soon learn that if she doesn't do her part, you won't let movies be a part of her recreational activities. This will help her be more grateful when she does get to go.

Teach Them to Be Second

Children should experience the joy of being second. This should be an everyday part of your routine. For instance, helping children to give the first part of the snack to their siblings ensures that they will likely do so for others later in life. Helping a child to let another sibling take a bath first is helping a child to learn to be considerate of others. Teaching a child to wait for a minute for your attention while you finish a phone conversation has benefits unnumbered.

However, it is best to teach children this particular skill first on a practice basis, not when the actual situation arises. You might pull a reluctant child aside and indicate,

> "Today is Michelle's birthday. I know that it is your day to take your bath first, but one way to celebrate Michelle's birthday is to offer her the chance to get into the tub first. Would you be willing to wait until the second turn today?"

> "We are having brownies for our treat tonight, but let's wait and give Dad the first piece when he gets home from work. It will be so fun to see his face when he knows we waited for him."

There are many adults who have never learned to be second. They must be the first one to open family Christmas presents; they sneak a bit of ice cream before it is served to the family on special occasions; they have to taste the dinner before the company arrives. They were apparently never taught the "I'll be happy to be second" skill. How you bless your children when you have taught them to let another in line first, to open a door for someone and enter afterward, and to wait for another to do something first. If you help them practice this in small areas, they will be more willing to be second when it comes to more important situations.

How wonderful are teenagers who can hold off self-gratification in front of their peers because they grew up in households where they gave other family members first choice. How strong are the characters of children who grow into adulthood knowing that waiting is good, beneficial, and a necessary part of life. Teach your children to wait long enough to be second to help them feel more grateful and generous.

Teach Them to Say Thank You a Second Time

Another way to increase contentment is to teach children how to say thank you in a more formal manner. Children who are taught to verbally say thank you, to write thank-you notes, and to otherwise express their gratitude more than once for the small, special pleasures of life will learn to have greater contentment and joy with their current circumstances.

More than any other skill, this is one that is observed by children as they interact and watch their parents. When you say "thank you" when your spouse helps you put on your coat, when you express gratitude for the delicious meal as it is served, when you stop to pray in gratitude after narrowly avoiding an accident, you are teaching your children to be grateful.

Of course, along with your example, you teach thank-you behavior by encouraging your children to express gratitude.

> "Jonah, you will want to say thank you when you get a birthday gift in the mail. Here is a fun thank-you card. I'll help you write a short note to Aunt Sarah. Then we can address it and send it off in tomorrow's mail. I know that you told her thank you when she called, but saying thank you twice is nice!"

Modeling Gratitude

When you are driving, working, playing, or just visiting, say thank you to your children for what they mean to you, what they do that pleases you, and how they act that makes you proud. Write them a thank-you note occasionally. These expression will reinforce their good behavior and also model gratitude behaviors for their own lives.

Naturally, children should be taught very early to pray and express their gratitude to their Heavenly Father for all that he has given them.

You may have met children who tend to be pessimistic and negative in their attitudes: "This isn't right; that isn't working; these things are not correct; the sky is grey, again." You will most likely see the same attitudes expressed when you meet their parents. So the question is, what do you want your children to grow up to be like? I would think that being content would be of great benefit in their lives, the crowning attitude you as a parent could instill in them.

These and other parenting skills are learned, shared, and nurtured as you try new skills, practice again and again, and then begin to see results. Remember, raising a child is a lifetime occupation. May your children turn out to be the way you want them to be no matter how they are now!

Conclusion

If I could leave a legacy for my children, it would be the capacity to function at a high level of independence, to work hard, and to love well. These are not attributes that come easily in adulthood. They are modeled from the time of the child's birth, taught at every opportunity, and then expected in rudimentary form from children at an early age. As experience and time allow, more complex and difficult tasks are added to the children's repertoire of achievements so that with each new challenge these values of independence, a strong work ethic, and the capacity to love and serve spring forth without thought. They have become part of your children's characters. They become independent, hardworking, and kind.

I remember holding my first son during those first few minutes after his birth and dreaming of what I wanted him to be like in twenty years. Of course, that emotional event was repeated again and again as each of our children came into our lives. I wanted them to be someone special. As I reviewed parenting books, carefully watched other families, and pondered my own past, I realized that this was going to be the work of a lifetime. It needed to start right away. I would be nurturing for many years. It wouldn't be easy and I would need to be very diligent and observant. I would also need to become what I wanted them to be, so I activated change in my own life.

Now that my children are grown and gone, for the most part I have few regrets. I wish I had been a little slower to discipline until softness could return to my voice. I wish I had been more understanding when they did something really annoying, but which didn't turn out to be serious. I wish I had been more patient when they made mistakes. But then, every parent has these regrets.

For the rest, I feel that it went well. My husband and I worked hard to teach them to obey. We gave them regular jobs so they knew how to work. We engendered a curiosity about life and a love of reading into their very bones. They are on their own now, the first a doctor of mathematics education, the second seeking a medical degree, the third on his way to getting a doctorate of computer science, and the fourth following his love of animation and film production and seeking a degree with those pursuits in mind. An intelligent, hardworking daughter has joined our family through marriage, and we now have our first grandson, so the patterns will soon be repeating themselves in the next generation.

Oh, parenting is a lifelong occupation. Even now I call and inquire after my children; occasionally I suggest and prod. Still, I hope and dream. So will you. To be a parent or to nurture a child in any capacity brings a fulfillment and joy like few other pursuits.

As you become more experienced with raising the children you desire to find joy in, please feel free to write me at marie@houseoforder .com with your own comments and opinions. I will add appropriate information into future editions of this book. This will help all of us teach and train our children for their brighter tomorrows.

Acknowledgments

A book, especially of this depth and kind, takes a lot of hearts and heads. My special thanks goes to the staff at Deseret Book, including Jana Erickson, my product director and continued mentor; Leslie Stitt, my editor and new friend; Heather Ward, my designer whose creativity I desire to emulate; and Rachael Ward, my typesetter whose accuracy warrants special note.

Thanks to my House of Order friends, whose number grows as I teach and travel. They have taught me, shared with me, and tutored me. They have also shown me new dimensions from their own lives and experiences about teaching children to work. They have expanded my own vision of what matters most in helping young people gain skills and how these principles should best be approached.

Lastly, I say thank you to my immediate family circle including my husband, Jim, and our four sons, Tom, David, Brian, and Tyler, and now our daughter-in-law, Jennifer, and our first grandchild, Timothy.

Each, in his or her own way, has been an important part of this book. Thanks again!

Index

~~~~~~~~~~~~~~~~~~~~~~~~~~~~~

About the Author

Marie Calder Ricks has been sharing home and professional organization skills for more than twenty-four years. She began teaching in
1986 at her local community education center where she developed an
eight-week, sixteen-topic course on personal organization, time management, food preparation, office and storage organization, budgeting, training children to work, and purchasing skills. Her classes have
proven popular both in California and Utah, where she now lives. She
frequently teaches organization principles at professional, church, and
community gatherings all over the United States.

Marie does personal consultations and she has prepared many
printed materials to help home managers and professionals get more
organized, whatever their needs may be.

Marie writes for various venues and appears as a featured guest on
both TV and radio. She has been a radio show host and is the owner
of House of Order, a company dedicated to helping men and women
everywhere find greater organization skills, both in their personal and
professional lives. She shares a weekly organization newsletter with

interested parties. Sign up on her informative and useful Web page, www.houseoforder.com.

Marie also has interests in many other areas. She loves to scrap quilt, make pressed-flower greeting cards for friends and family, and write personal histories.

She is happily married to Jim Ricks and they are the parents of five sons. She and her husband live in Highland, Utah.

Praise for Marie Calder Ricks!

"I learned a method of praising children from you: specific praise. I decided to try it out on my six-year-old son. I had him vacuum the bathroom rug. He did the job willingly and then came to tell me he was finished. I took a look and said, 'Wow, Ben, that rug looks like it is brand new!' instead of my usual, 'Good job, buddy. Thanks!' That child's buttons just about burst off his shirt, and his whole face lit up. Then he said the words that shocked me, 'What else can I do, Mom?'"

—Jessica R.

"Your information is so helpful and is presented in such a fun and easy-to-understand format! I went home last night with even more ideas to improve upon, and I am excited to get started! Thank you for the much-needed validation and understanding."

—Callae W.

"Thank you so much for your time, inspiration, and insights to help my life be more organized. . . . You were an answer to prayer!"

—Robbi K.

"My home and life are much better, and I feel great! You have a gift and left me feeling motivated and capable!"

—Becky K.

"Thank you so much for sharing your time and talents with women everywhere. I have made a lot of improvements as a result. Thank you for sharing your wisdom and personal experiences so freely."

—Jill S.

"Because your system is so detailed, my friend understood it right away and is ready to give it a try. She loves the step-by-step approach to parenting and how clear the instructions are. She phoned her sister this morning telling her how excited she was with your program."

—Irene H.